Editor
Eric Migliaccio

Illustrator
Clint McKnight

Cover Artist
Brenda DiAntonis

Managing Editor
Ina Massler Levin, M.A.

Creative Director
Karen J. Goldfluss, M.S. Ed.

Art Production Manager
Kevin Barnes

Art Coordinator
Renée Christine Yates

Imaging
Rosa C. See

Publisher

Mary D. Smith, M.S. Ed.

Vocabulary Words In Context

Grades 6-8

101 L...

The lake's surface was **serene** and reflective.

The wet **frond** glistened in the sun.

Includes
Over 600 Words
in a Variety of Contexts
- Newspaper Articles
- Friendly Letters
- Fliers
- Advertisements
- Recipes
- Riddles

Includes
Standards &
Benchmarks

MW00475130

Author

Margaret Brinton

Teacher Created Resources, Inc.
12621 Western Avenue
Garden Grove, CA 92841
www.teachercreated.com

ISBN: 978-1-4206-8143-7

©*2007 Teacher Created Resources, Inc.*
Reprinted, 2018
Made in U.S.A.

Teacher Created Resources

Table of Contents

Table of Contents *(cont.)*

Standards

101 Lessons: Vocabulary Words in Context meets the following language-arts standards and benchmarks for the Grades 6–8 classroom. (Used with permission from McREL. Copyright 2004 McREL. Mid-continent Research for Education and Learning. 2550 S. Parker Road, Suite 500, Aurora, CO 80014. Telephone: (303) 337-0990. Website: *www.mcrel.org/standards-benchmarks.*)

Standards 5: Uses the general skills and strategies of the reading process

- Establishes and adjusts purposes for reading (e.g., to understand, interpret, enjoy, solve problems, predict outcomes, answer a specific question, form an opinion, skim for facts; to discover models for own writing)

- Uses word origins and derivations to understand word meaning (e.g., Latin and Greek roots and affixes, meanings of foreign words frequently used in the English language, historical influences on English word meanings)

- Uses a variety of strategies to extend reading vocabulary (e.g., uses analogies, idioms, similes, metaphors to infer the meaning of literal and figurative phrases; uses definition, restatement, example, comparison and contrast to verify word meanings; identifies shades of meaning; knows denotative and connotative meanings; knows vocabulary related to different content areas and current events; uses rhyming dictionaries, classification books, etymological dictionaries)

Introduction

There are many vocabulary books designed to introduce students to the complex world of words that the English language has to offer. Harder to find, however, are resources that show students how and when to use those words correctly. *101 Lessons: Using Vocabulary in Context* takes the learning process that one step further by giving students the more complete comprehension they need in order to accurately use over 600 vocabulary words in their writing and speech.

Each of the 101 lessons in this book is comprised of three parts:

Section I: Context

The first section of each lesson features a written piece that contains the vocabulary words. Because the words fit comfortably within the context of the piece, students are able to see an example of the correct usage of each word.

Several different written formats are used in this section. One piece may be in the form of a newspaper article, while the next is in that of an advertisement or personal letter. The lessons span the genres, with nonfiction accounts of the extraordinary included alongside fictitious tales of the everyday. In this way, students are able to better understand all of the contexts in which words and language are employed.

In this first section, students participate in the piece in one of two ways:

1. Students are given a list of definitions and asked to match the correct definition with its corresponding word in the piece. Students must use context clues from the piece to determine which definition fits which word.

2. Students are given a mini dictionary, which is a list of vocabulary words and their definitions. The students are then asked to complete the piece by using those words to fill in the blanks. In this type of exercise, students need to understand the context in order to plug in the correct words.

Section II: Repetition

The second section of each lesson gives students a chance to practice the spelling of their new vocabulary words. Students rewrite each word three times. This repetition gives students a sense of familiarity with the words and helps them commit the words to memory.

Section III: Reinforcement

The third section features an activity that reinforces students' understanding of the words. This section offers several formats, including analogies, context clues, fill-in-the-blanks, matching, synonyms and antonyms, etc.

For ease of use, an answer key is provided on pages 106–109. Also, a complete index of the vocabulary words taught in this book is given on pages 110–112.

The Family Fisherman

Directions: Find the meaning of each underlined word in the paragraph below. Put the letter of the answer on the blank line to the left. Use the definitions in the box below to help you.

> A. dark and unclear
>
> B. occupation, job
>
> C. fisherman
>
> D. attract
>
> E. natural talent
>
> F. to throw

1. _____
2. _____
3. _____
4. _____
5. _____
6. _____

I live with my mom and step-dad. We live near a river, and we eat a lot of catfish. That's because my step-dad is an **1**angler. When he fishes, he likes to catch one that is big enough for our dinner. He doesn't bother to bring the small ones home: he will just **2**fling those back into the water. What does he use to **3**entice the fish? Well, a fat worm, of course! Somehow, even in a **4**murky river, a fish can find a worm! I guess my step-dad really has a **5**flair for fishing. He never comes home without at least one fat catfish. Maybe fishing should be his full-time **6**vocation!

Directions: Spell each new word three times.

1. angler   _____   _____   _____

2. fling   _____   _____   _____

3. entice   _____   _____   _____

4. murky   _____   _____   _____

5. flair   _____   _____   _____

6. vocation   _____   _____   _____

Activity: Put your new words in ABC order. Then, next to each word, write the meaning.

1. _____   _____

2. _____   _____

3. _____   _____

4. _____   _____

5. _____   _____

6. _____   _____

A Letter From Camp Pine

Directions: Find the meaning of each underlined word in the friendly letter below. Put the letter of the answer on the blank line to the left. Use the definitions in the box below to help you.

> A. *to enjoy some warmth*
> B. *a defending wall*
> C. *very frightened*
> D. *a type of leaf*
> E. *a warning of trouble*
> F. *a loyal trust*

1. _____

2. _____

3. _____

4. _____

5. _____

6. _____

Hello, Aunt Tracy! I promised I would write to you from camp. Well, here I am! The group in my cabin is a friendly group, and we have promised an [1]allegiance to each other.

I found something pretty on our hike yesterday. It was a [2]frond, and my counselor said I could bring it back to the cabin. I saw something horrible, too. It was a huge scorpion, and I felt completely [3]aghast. It was a great day to hike, though. The sun was bright, and our whole group wanted to take a break and [4]bask. A [5]portent of a thunderstorm later in the day forced us to return to the cabins.

You do not need to worry about my safety. The campground is surrounded by a [6]rampart.

Directions: Spell each new word three times.

1. allegiance _____ _____ _____

2. frond _____ _____ _____

3. aghast _____ _____ _____

4. bask _____ _____ _____

5. portent _____ _____ _____

6. rampart _____ _____ _____

Activity: Put your new words in ABC order. Then, next to each word, write the meaning.

1. _____ _____

2. _____ _____

3. _____ _____

4. _____ _____

5. _____ _____

6. _____ _____

Kids Cookin' Out

Directions: Find the meaning of each underlined word in the invitation below. Put the letter of the answer on the blank line to the left. Use the definitions in the box below to help you.

> A. *a type of tree*
> B. *a little bit*
> C. *a rainwater ditch*
>
> D. *sociable*
> E. *skillfull*
> F. *territory*

1. _____
2. _____
3. _____
4. _____
5. _____
6. _____

All eighth graders in this neighborhood are invited to a cookout on Saturday at noon. Meet at the East baseball field. Be careful when you cross the [1]culvert: there is some flooding there. When you get to the field, come to the picnic table under the tallest [2]elm. That area will be our private [3]domain! This party is going to be a celebration of spring, so everyone needs to be in a [4]convivial mood! We need one volunteer who is very [5]deft at lighting a barbecue grill. We will serve plenty of hot dogs and catsup—with just a [6]smidgen of mustard!

Directions: Spell each new word three times.

1. culvert _____ _____ _____

2. elm _____ _____ _____

3. domain _____ _____ _____

4. convivial _____ _____ _____

5. deft _____ _____ _____

6. smidgen _____ _____ _____

Activity: Fill in the blanks in each sentence with your new word.

1. A large ____ ____ ____ a ____ ____ in England belongs to the royal family.

2. Exercise your body to become more ____ e ____ ____!

3. He found a dead fish near the ____ ____ ____ ____ ____ r ____.

4. I rested in the shade of the ____ ____ ____ .

5. Don't overdo it! A ____ ____ i ____ ____ e ____ is enough.

6. Let's eat, dance, and act ____ ____ ____ ____ i ____ i ____ ____!

Pocket the Cash!

Directions: Read the following posted reward. Find the meaning of each underlined word. Put the letter of the answer on the blank line. Use the definitions in the box below to help you.

> A. *a little cart*
>
> B. *a type of tree*
>
> C. *more than enough*
>
> D. *a meeting place*
>
> E. *to beg*
>
> F. *deserving blame*

REWARD!
Call Sally at 555–1011

1. _____

2. _____

3. _____

4. _____

5. _____

6. _____

Thirty dollars will be paid for the return of my lost backpack! It was last seen on the ground under the **¹aspen** in Tilly Park.

Stealing my backpack was a **²reprehensible** action, but I will forgive you and even reward you if you will just return it. What am I supposed to do without it: load my school supplies into a **³tumbrel**?

If you have my backpack, please call me and we can arrange a **⁴rendezvous** in front of my house. Thirty dollars is a **⁵plenteous** reward. I **⁶implore** you! Please return my backpack!

Directions: Spell each new word three times.

1. aspen _____ _____ _____

2. reprehensible _____ _____ _____

3. tumbrel _____ _____ _____

4. rendezvous _____ _____ _____

5. plenteous _____ _____ _____

6. implore _____ _____ _____

Activity: Circle the best answer to each of the following questions.

1. Which one brings people together?   **rendezvous** or **plenteous**

2. Which one is a manufactured product?   **aspen** or **tumbrel**

3. Which one is a strong action?   **tumbrel** or **implore**

4. Which one produces oxygen?   **plenteous** or **aspen**

5. Which one means "awful"?   **reprehensible** or **implore**

6. Which means "not lacking"?   **plenteous** or **rendezvous**

A Winter's Sleep

Directions: Use the mini dictionary to fill in the missing words in the paragraph below.

> *clad — to be dressed*
> *piedmont — base of a mountain*
> *rouse — to bring to action*
>
> *sedentary — inactive*
> *bruin — a bear*
> *cumbersome — heavy and bulky*

As autumn changes to winter, a (**1.**) _____ is
preparing to sleep. His winter sleep will be long and deep. Is it because
he is lazy, or is it because he is large and (**2.**) _____
and just needs to rest his big body? In any case, he goes to sleep without a blanket.
He is (**3.**) _____ only in his own fur. During
his long winter's sleep, he is totally (**4.**) _____ .
Nothing will (**5.**) _____ him. Finally, as winter is
passing and the freshness of spring is in the air, he begins to wake up. He stretches
and roars. Then he exits his cave and takes a look at the world from the
(**6.**) _____

Directions: Spell each new word three times.

1. clad _____ _____ _____
2. piedmont _____ _____ _____
3. rouse _____ _____ _____
4. sedentary _____ _____ _____
5. bruin _____ _____ _____
6. cumbersome _____ _____ _____

Activity: Write the best new word in the blank for each idea.

1. not active at all _____
2. a large, furry animal _____
3. to wake up _____
4. with clothes on _____
5. not the peak _____
6. not easy or light _____

Let Your Mind Work

Directions: Use the mini dictionary to answer the riddles below.

> *countenance — expression on a face*
> *bard — a singing poet*
> *tirade — a stormy attack of words*
> *panacea — the cure for all troubles*
>
> *javelin — a light spear*
> *steward — a kitchen manager*
> *fissure — deep crack*
> *vanguard — the forward movement in the arts*

_____ 1. I am the result of a large earthquake.

_____ 2. I am in charge of meals and menus on a large ship.

_____ 3. I could be used for hunting small animals.

_____ 4. I am all of your anger let out.

_____ 5. I am the lead in a new style of music.

_____ 6. I am the final solution.

_____ 7. I am known for my verses.

_____ 8. I am a sign of your feelings.

Directions: Spell each new word three times.

1. countenance _____ _____ _____

2. bard _____ _____ _____

3. tirade _____ _____ _____

4. panacea _____ _____ _____

5. javelin _____ _____ _____

6. steward _____ _____ _____

7. fissure _____ _____ _____

8. vanguard _____ _____ _____

Activity: Complete each sentence with the best new word.

1. The hostess paid a _____ to entertain the guests.

2. There is no medicine that is an absolute _____ .

3. There would never be new creations without a _____ .

4. Always start each new day with a positive _____ .

5. We saw water coming out of the _____ .

6. A _____ was often used by Native Americans.

7. The ship's _____ launched an angry _____ at the lazy cook.

Wooly Winter Wear

Directions: Read the following clothing advertisement. Find each underlined word. Find the matching meaning in the box of definitions below and place the letter on the line next to the word.

> A. to hurry
> B. relief from something
> C. fireside
> D. a set
> E. supply of things
> F. gloomy

Buy Your Winter Clothes Now!

_____ 1. a bright red sweater for gray and <u>dismal</u> winter days: $19.00

_____ 2. a stylish jacket to keep you warm as you <u>bustle</u> about: $48.00

_____ 3. fuzzy slippers to give your feet <u>succor</u> after ice skating: $12.00

_____ 4. a nice <u>ensemble</u> of matching hat and mittens: $15.00

_____ 5. a heavy robe to put on when you sit by the warm <u>hearth</u>: $20.00

_____ 6. thick socks to add to your <u>repertory</u> of winter footwear: $3.50

Directions: Spell each new word three times.

1. dismal _____ _____ _____

2. bustle _____ _____ _____

3. succor _____ _____ _____

4. ensemble _____ _____ _____

5. hearth _____ _____ _____

6. repertory _____ _____ _____

Activity: Identify each of the following ideas with one of your new words.

1. products ready to sell _____

2. not so cheerful _____

3. a cozy place _____

4. American Red Cross provides this. _____

5. Don't delay! _____

6. a nice color blend of clothing _____

Life in a Lighthouse

Directions: Read the following tale from a lighthouse keeper. Find the meaning of each underlined word. Put the letter of the answer on the blank line to the left.

> A. *hidden rock*
> B. *wide view*
> C. *peaceful*
> D. *broken down*
> E. *loyal, steady*
> F. *lonely*

1. _____
2. _____
3. _____
4. _____
5. _____
6. _____

Welcome to my home, the lighthouse. Yes, I actually live here with my wife and child. We love living here on the edge of the sea because, from our front window, we have a wonderful [1]sweep of the water. It was a [2]ramshackle lighthouse when we moved in, but we've fixed it up, and it's very comfortable now! We have a good life here. For some people, living here would be [3]forlorn. We actually enjoy the peace and quiet. Unless there is a storm at sea, our life here is very [4]serene. My job is very important, too. From the beam of the light, ships come safely home. Without the light, it would be easy to scrape against a [5]skerry. To a ship's captain, a lighthouse keeper like me is a [6]staid friend.

Directions: Spell each new word three times.

1. sweep _____ _____ _____
2. ramshackle _____ _____ _____
3. forlorn _____ _____ _____
4. serene _____ _____ _____
5. skerry _____ _____ _____
6. staid _____ _____ _____

Activity: Circle the best answer to each question.

1. Which is an empty feeling? **staid** or **forlorn**
2. Which is hard and rough? **sweep** or **skerry**
3. Which means "quiet"? **serene** or **ramshackle**
4. Which means "trustworthy"? **skerry** or **staid**
5. Which is a moving sight? **sweep** or **forlorn**
6. Which is not nice and new? **ramshackle** or **serene**

      12

A Huge One

Directions: Use the mini dictionary to fill in the missing words in the paragraph below.

> *prowess — superior skill*
> *loll — to be lazy*
> *celestial — by the moon and stars*
>
> *erratic — irregular*
> *leviathan — a huge sea creature*
> *maelstrom— a violent whirlpool*

There is more than one (**1.**) _____ that swims in the sea. In fact, there are groups of them that migrate from Alaska to Mexico each year. Because it is a long journey, they (**2.**) _____ in the warm waters of Mexico before they return to Alaska. There is nothing (**3.**) _____ about their journey. By instinct they know their course, and they stick to it. Many people wonder if the leviathans use (**4.**) _____ navigation because they seem to find their way even through a (**5.**) _____ . We can respect the leviathans and their natural (**6.**) _____ to swim in the sea.

Directions: Spell each new word three times.

1. prowess _____ _____ _____

2. loll _____ _____ _____

3. celestial _____ _____ _____

4. erratic _____ _____ _____

5. leviathan _____ _____ _____

6. maelstrom _____ _____ _____

Activity: On the blank line, write the best new word for each idea.

1. a telescope's view _____

2. swirling water _____

3. uneven _____

4. one way to relax _____

5. a sea creature _____

6. a champion needs this _____

To the Rescue

Directions: Imagine that you are a member of the U.S. Coast Guard. This is the emergency call that you receive. Find the meaning of each underlined word. Put the letter of the answer on the blank line to the left. Use the definitions in the box below to help you.

> A. *to climb with difficulty*   D. *deep, deep place*
>
> B. *unsteady light*   E. *false idea*
>
> C. *to ruin, spoil*   F. *wide ray of light*

1. _____
2. _____
3. _____
4. _____
5. _____
6. _____

"Help! Help! This is a real call for help! This is no **1**<u>illusion</u>! We are just west of San Francisco Bay, and we are sinking fast! In a few more minutes, our boat will go down into the **2**<u>abyss</u>! We are going to try to **3**<u>clamber</u> aboard a tiny raft. Our timing is important — let's hope we don't **4**<u>botch</u> our plan! It's getting dark fast! Please search for us with your **5**<u>floodlight</u>! You'll need more than a **6**<u>flicker</u>! Come quickly! Help! Help!"

Directions: Spell each new word three times.

1. illusion   _____   _____   _____

2. abyss   _____   _____   _____

3. clamber   _____   _____   _____

4. botch   _____   _____   _____

5. floodlight   _____   _____   _____

6. flicker   _____   _____   _____

Activity: Decide if the following pairs are synonyms or antonyms. Write **S** (for synonym) or **A** (for *antonym*) on each blank line.

_____ 1. reality   illusion   _____ 4. beam   floodlight

_____ 2. pit   abyss   _____ 5. blaze   flicker

_____ 3. succeed   botch   _____ 6. clamber   slide

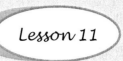
The Game of Golf

Directions: Find the meaning of each underlined word in the paragraph below. Put the letter of the answer on the blank line to the left. Use the definitions in the box below to help you.

> A. *of excellent tradition*
>
> B. *not yet developed*
>
> C. *to be dressed*
>
> D. *a cause to annoy*
>
> E. *to handle very well*
>
> F. *bright and energetic*

Community Golf League Now Forming!

1. _____
2. _____
3. _____
4. _____
5. _____
6. _____

Girl golfers wanted! Ages 10–14. We want experienced players and also those with **1**latent skills. We will teach you the correct swings. You will soon learn to **2**wield each different club.

Our first meeting will be April 4th at 5 P.M. at Perry Park. Come **3**attired in a nice shirt and pants. Blue jeans are not allowed. Come also with a great amount of patience because learning golf can be a **4**vexation.

Let's have fun! Bring a **5**vibrant attitude! Come learn this **6**classic sport.

Directions: Spell each new word three times.

1. latent _____ _____ _____

2. wield _____ _____ _____

3. attired _____ _____ _____

4. vexation _____ _____ _____

5. vibrant _____ _____ _____

6. classic _____ _____ _____

Activity: On the line next to each idea, write the letter of the matching word.

_____ 1. in suit and tie   A. vibrant

_____ 2. something that frustrates   B. classic

_____ 3. not dull   C. latent

_____ 4. a good, old style   D. attired

_____ 5. to use with an ability   E. wield

_____ 6. almost ready to grow or show   F. vexation

Skinny Wheels

Directions: Read the "Bike for Sale!" notice below. Use the mini dictionary to help you write the correct word in each blank.

> *emulate — to try to equal*
> *gaudy — overly bright*
> *dapper — stylish*
> *wrought — formed from metal*
> *regret — a sad feeling for a mistake*
> *jubilant — joyful*

Bike for Sale!

Wonderful three-speed bicycle for sale — carefully (**1.**) _____ from high-quality aluminum. This bike is so exciting to ride that you will feel (**2.**) _____ each time you use it! Your friends will be jealous and will want to (**3.**) _____ you. It is a nice red color, but it is not (**4.**) _____. You will look very (**5.**) _____ riding it. Just $120.00! If you don't buy it, you'll be filled with (**6.**) _____.

Directions: Spell each new word three times.

1. emulate _____ _____ _____

2. gaudy _____ _____ _____

3. dapper _____ _____ _____

4. wrought _____ _____ _____

5. regret _____ _____ _____

6. jubilant _____ _____ _____

Activity: Match each idea to the correct word. Place the letter of the answer in the blank.

_____ 1. created by shaping   A. emulate

_____ 2. with too much makeup   B. gaudy

_____ 3. to copy in a nice way   C. dapper

_____ 4. looking very good   D. wrought

_____ 5. A nice surprise makes you feel this way!   E. regret

_____ 6. not a good feeling   F. jubilant

I Caught a Cold

Directions: Find the meaning of each underlined word in the paragraph below. Put the letter of the answer on the blank line to the left. Use the definitions in the box below to help you.

> A. *a clear understanding*   D. *a drugstore*
>
> B. *terrible, drastic*   E. *strong and healthy*
>
> C. *physical illness*   F. *a good rest*

1. _____
2. _____
3. _____
4. _____
5. _____
6. _____

Last month, I caught a very bad cold. When I went to see my doctor, she said, "I am sending you to the **1**apothecary. Your health condition is **2**dire." I always trust my doctor's advice. Regarding my health, she always has **3**insight. So, after I picked up my medicine, I returned home and went to bed for two days. That **4**respite and the medicine cured me! Within 48 hours, I was beginning to feel **5**vigorous again. I had recovered from my **6**infirmity.

Directions: Spell each new word three times.

1. apothecary   _____   _____   _____
2. dire   _____   _____   _____
3. insight   _____   _____   _____
4. respite   _____   _____   _____
5. vigorous   _____   _____   _____
6. infirmity   _____   _____   _____

Activity: Draw a line to match each idea with the best new word.

1. really horrible   A. apothecary
2. sickness   B. dire
3. a time to recover   C. insight
4. medication is sold here   D. respite
5. a wise knowledge   E. vigorous
6. full of energy   F. infirmity

A New Kind of Schooling

Directions: The information below is from the Old West School. For each underlined word, put the letter of the answer on the blank line to the left. Use the definitions in the box to help you.

> A. skillful
> B. short riding pants
> C. a small disaster
> D. disgust, dislike
> E. cowboys
> F. continuing effort

1. _____
2. _____
3. _____
4. _____
5. _____
6. _____

"Welcome to the Old West School for **1**Wranglers. At our school, it is important that each of you learn to ride a horse. So, I hope that nobody has an **2**aversion to horses. You're going to be spending a lot of time around them.

"Now, about your clothing. You are all going to need very tough jeans. I don't want anybody showing up in **3**breeches! We'll practice riding horses every day, and you'll eventually become **4**adroit. But it's going to take a lot of patience and **5**perseverance. Our goal is to keep you on your horse's back, because falling off would sure be a **6**calamity."

Directions: Spell each new word three times.

1. wranglers _____ _____ _____
2. aversion _____ _____ _____
3. breeches _____ _____ _____
4. adroit _____ _____ _____
5. perseverance _____ _____ _____
6. calamity _____ _____ _____

Activity: Fill in the blanks by using your new words.

1. A jockey wears boots and _____ for every horse race.
2. Losing my wallet while on vacation was a _____ .
3. To pitch a ball well, a player must be _____ .
4. Big, black spiders give me a feeling of _____ .
5. _____ work on cattle ranches.
6. With _____ , I can learn anything.

Jurassic Genes

Directions: Read the information below about the dinosaur age known as the Jurassic Period. Find the meaning of each underlined word. Put the letter of the answer on the blank line. Use the definitions in the box below to help you.

> A. *to yield the power*
> B. *long periods of history*
> C. *friendly*
>
> D. *feast*
> E. *courage*
> F. *a small canyon*

1. _____
2. _____
3. _____
4. _____
5. _____
6. _____

Put your imagination millions of **1**eons back in time to the Jurassic Period when dinosaurs lived. Now let's picture that marvelous monster, apatosaurus! Because he did not eat meat, he was a little more **2**amiable than some of the other monsters of that period. His huge weight and size, however, made the smaller dinosaurs **3**defer to him. Only creatures with a lot of **4**gumption dared to approach him! Apatosaurus spent most of his time in the water, chewing on plants and leaves. Green, growing things provided his **5**repast. To finish his meal, he drank from a rain-filled **6**gully!

Directions: Spell each new word three times.

1. eons   _____   _____   _____
2. amiable _____   _____   _____
3. defer   _____   _____   _____
4. gumption _____   _____   _____
5. repast   _____   _____   _____
6. gully   _____   _____   _____

Activity: Cross out the word in each group that does not belong.

1. nice	amiable	mean	agreeable
2. bravery	strength	gumption	intelligence
3. banquet	task	repast	celebration
4. prairie	ditch	gully	valley
5. eons	ages	fortunes	centuries
6. resist	defer	submit	give in

I Must Remind Myself

Directions: Find the meaning of each underlined word in the paragraph below. Put the letter of the answer on the blank line. Use the definitions in the box below to help you.

> A. *a strict person*
>
> B. *to appear angry*
>
> C. *sneaky, tricky*
>
> D. *to disagree*
>
> E. *bad words*
>
> F. *posture*

1. _____
2. _____
3. _____
4. _____
5. _____
6. _____

I must always sit and walk in an important way. I will practice my [1]carriage every day. I will put a smile upon my face. It does not look friendly to [2]sulk. I will never use [3]invectives in my speaking or writing. I will become more of a [4]stickler about getting my homework done. I will try not to [5]clash with my parents; I will respect their ideas, instead. I must always be honest and never [6]insidious. Honesty is the best policy!

Directions: Spell each new word three times.

1. carriage _____ _____ _____

2. sulk _____ _____ _____

3. invectives _____ _____ _____

4. stickler _____ _____ _____

5. clash _____ _____ _____

6. insidious _____ _____ _____

Activity: First, put all of your new words in ABC order. Then, next to each word, write its meaning.

1. _____ _____

2. _____ _____

3. _____ _____

4. _____ _____

5. _____ _____

6. _____ _____

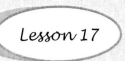

Pups and Pooches

Directions: Find the meaning of each word in the paragraph below. Put the letter of the answer on the blank line. Use the definitions in the box below to help you.

> A. *to drink deeply*
> B. *not attractive*
> C. *hostile, unfriendly*
> D. *overeater*
> E. *to give relief*
> F. *type of wild bird*

A+ Dog Care Service (Call Mike: 555-1272)

_____ 1. We will <u>alleviate</u> your dog's boredom by walking him twice a day.

_____ 2. We will feed him daily and provide plenty of water for him to <u>quaff</u>.

_____ 3. If he has a <u>bellicose</u> character, we will calm him down.

_____ 4. We will keep him on a healthy diet and not allow him to become a <u>glutton</u>.

_____ 5. If his fur is <u>unsightly</u>, we will clip him and clean him.

_____ 6. We will even teach him how to hunt <u>pheasant</u>, if you like.

Directions: Spell each new word three times.

1. alleviate _____ _____ _____

2. quaff _____ _____ _____

3. bellicose _____ _____ _____

4. glutton _____ _____ _____

5. unsightly _____ _____ _____

6. pheasant _____ _____ _____

Activity: On the line next to each idea, write the letter of the matching word.

_____ 1. when a sight is not pretty　　A. alleviate

_____ 2. to smooth out the problem　　B. bellicose

_____ 3. like a hungry pig　　C. quaff

_____ 4. put down the throat　　D. glutton

_____ 5. not very friendly　　E. unsightly

_____ 6. You can cook this.　　F. pheasant

It Was Not a Good Ride

Directions: Use the mini dictionary to help you fill in the missing words in the story below.

> *blithe — cheerful*
> *queasy — sick to the stomach*
> *stow — to put away*
>
> *fruition — complete satisfaction*
> *pall — a gloomy expression*
> *actuate — to put into action*

I had been so excited! I was going to take my first sailboat ride, and I was filled with happiness. I boarded my uncle's boat with my picnic lunch and a jug of juice to (**1.**) _____ under my seat. Unfortunately, my boat ride was not what I had expected. The wind was so strong that the movement made me feel (**2.**) _____. I had started out so (**3.**) _____, but now I was miserable. My uncle was worried because of the (**4.**) _____ on my face. After only one hour on the bay, he said, "I will put the sails down, and I will (**5.**) _____ the motor. We will be back at the dock in just five minutes." We got back to the dock safely, but I was disappointed that my ride on the boat did not come to (**6.**) _____ .

Directions: Spell each new word three times.

1. blithe   _____   _____   _____

2. queasy   _____   _____   _____

3. stow   _____   _____   _____

4. fruition   _____   _____   _____

5. pall   _____   _____   _____

6. actuate   _____   _____   _____

Activity: On a sheet of your own paper, copy the story by filling in all missing words.

Teacher Talk

Directions: Find the meaning of each underlined word in the sentences below. Put the letter of the answer on the blank line. Use the definitions in the box below to help you.

A. *to customize in a particular way*	D. *to go beyond*
B. *to make a list*	E. *to stay longer*
C. *to use a little color*	F. *to laugh and giggle*

_____ 1. On your biology drawings, always <u>tinge</u> the drawings lightly.

_____ 2. Do not <u>titter</u> during class. Have fun with your friends during your breaks.

_____ 3. When you are working in the library, <u>tarry</u> there until you are done.

_____ 4. For your math project, <u>tailor</u> it exactly to your personal interest.

_____ 5. When you are working with your math facts, <u>tabulate</u> them.

_____ 6. Each day, try harder to <u>transcend</u> what you already know.

Directions: Spell each new word three times.

1. tinge _____ _____ _____

2. titter _____ _____ _____

3. tarry _____ _____ _____

4. tailor _____ _____ _____

5. tabulate _____ _____ _____

6. transcend _____ _____ _____

Activity: Decide if the following pairs are synonyms or antonyms. Write **S** (for *synonym*) or **A** (for *antonym*) on each blank.

_____ 1. tinge	tint		_____ 4. tailor	goof up
_____ 2. titter	sob		_____ 5. tabulate	erase
_____ 3. tarry	linger		_____ 6. transcend	fail

Where Is Big Foot Now?

Directions: Find the meaning of each underlined word in the paragraph below. Put the letter of the answer on the blank line. Use the definitions in the box below to help you.

> A. evil
> B. to roam all around
> C. careless
> D. a form of transportation
> E. a member of a habitat
> F. to cleverly avoid

1. _____
2. _____
3. _____
4. _____
5. _____
6. _____

People say that Big Foot **1**rambles through the woods. He has very big feet, and he uses them. No other **2**conveyance is necessary! People have seen his shadow in Oregon. Others have reported seeing him in Canada. People believe that Big Foot is a beast, but not **3**malevolent. Although nobody has been harmed by Big Foot, it would still be **4**feckless to approach him. The best policy seems to be "Keep your distance." So far, Big Foot has always been able to **5**elude those who search for him. He is a **6**denizen of thick, dark forests, and the woods provide his cover.

Directions: Spell each new word three times.

1. ramble   _____   _____   _____
2. conveyance _____   _____   _____
3. malevolent _____   _____   _____
4. feckless   _____   _____   _____
5. elude   _____   _____   _____
6. denizen   _____   _____   _____

Activity: Fill in the blanks with your new words.

1. "Escape" is similar to _____.

2. A cart or a carriage is a _____.

3. A violent character is very _____.

4. A way to walk around is _____.

5. Reckless is like _____.

6. A creature of a place is a _____.

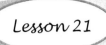

One Angry Blackbird

Directions: Read the following speech of a blackbird to a scarecrow. Find the meaning of each underlined word. Put the letter of the answer on the blank line. Use the definitions in the box below to help you.

A. *to bother, annoy*	D. *to stick out*
B. *a silly trick*	E. *a guard*
C. *mean, unkind*	F. *make a forward move*

1. _____

2. _____

3. _____

4. _____

5. _____

6. _____

Caw! Caw! Caw! What's that ugly thing doing in my cornfield? You don't suppose that is what they call a scarecrow? Huh! Well, it doesn't scare me! Hey, you **1**ornery thing! Stop waving your long arms around my face. That's my corn, you know. You can stop your **2**caper right now, and let me get my lunch! In fact, you are really beginning to **3**irk me. So, stop waving around like that. I'm about to **4**lunge at you and bite you if I don't get my lunch soon. Anyway, why does all of your hair **5**protrude like that? Haven't you heard of a comb? Now, here I come! You might think you are a **6**sentinel, but my desire for corn is stronger than my fear of you!

Directions: Spell each new word three times.

1. ornery _____ _____ _____

2. caper _____ _____ _____

3. irk _____ _____ _____

4. lunge _____ _____ _____

5. protrude _____ _____ _____

6. sentinel _____ _____ _____

Activity: Circle the best answer to each of the following questions.

1. Which would be another name for a watchdog? **caper** or **sentinel**

2. Which is an irritating behavior? **sentinel** or **irk**

3. Which might make you laugh? **caper** or **ornery**

4. Which is a movement? **ornery** or **lunge**

5. What is a bad attitude? **protrude** or **ornery**

6. Which action would not hide? **protrude** or **irk**

Toy Boat Tuesdays

Directions: Read the posted notice below. Find the meaning of each underlined word. Put the letter of the answer on the blank line. Use the definitions in the box below to help you.

> A. complete control   D. a continuous buzzing sound
>
> B. noisy crowd   E. shelter
>
> C. hobby   F. rowboat

1. _____

2. _____

3. _____

4. _____

5. _____

6. _____

The lake will be closed for regular boating every Tuesday. So keep your canoe or your **1**<u>dinghy</u> at home! Every Tuesday the lake is available for remote-controlled toy boats only! The ducks hate it and try to escape the noisy **2**<u>drone</u>; but toy boat operators love it! On Tuesdays, the whole lake is under their **3**<u>reign</u>.

The public is welcome to come and watch the fun. But, come quietly—we don't want the fun to be disturbed by a **4**<u>rabble</u>! On very windy days, the toy boat operators use the little bay on the north side of the lake as their **5**<u>lee</u>. Everyone is welcome to come and enjoy this popular **6**<u>avocation</u>.

Directions: Spell each new word three times.

1. dinghy   _____   _____   _____

2. drone   _____   _____   _____

3. reign   _____   _____   _____

4. rabble   _____   _____   _____

5. lee   _____   _____   _____

6. avocation   _____   _____   _____

Activity: Circle the clue word(s) in each sentence that helped you figure out the meaning of each new word. Then, decide if each of the following answers would be "Yes" or "No." Circle **Y** or **N**.

1. If in danger, could I hide in a lee?   **Y**   **N**

2. Is an avocation usually boring?   **Y**   **N**

3. Would a crowd of people fit in a dinghy?   **Y**   **N**

4. Might a football game attract a rabble?   **Y**   **N**

5. Would a swarm of flies create a drone?   **Y**   **N**

6. Could an ancient royal family have had a reign?   **Y**   **N**

Up for an Oscar

Directions: Read each of the following movie titles. Find the meaning of each underlined word and put the letter of the answer on the blank line. Use the definitions in the box below to help you.

> A. *sailboat race*   D. *difficult maze*
> B. *military fort*   E. *old horse*
> C. *destruction*   F. *daydream*

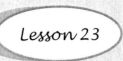

_____ 1. Civil War Battle at the <u>Garrison</u>

_____ 2. Romantic Teenage <u>Reverie</u>

_____ 3. Cowboy Saves His <u>Nag</u>

_____ 4. Earth's <u>Demolition</u> by Comet

_____ 5. Exciting <u>Regatta</u> Competition

_____ 6. Lost in the <u>Labyrinth</u>

Directions: Spell each new word three times.

1. garrison _____ _____ _____
2. reverie _____ _____ _____
3. nag _____ _____ _____
4. demolition _____ _____ _____
5. regatta _____ _____ _____
6. labyrinth _____ _____ _____

Activity: Cross out the word in each group that does not belong.

1. confusion	puzzle	simple	labyrinth
2. nag	mare	canine	stallion
3. task	imagination	reverie	fantasy
4. competition	regatta	event	election
5. purchase	guard	garrison	protect
6. disaster	demolition	duty	demolish

To Gather We Go

Directions: Find the meaning of each underlined word in the paragraph below. Put the letter of the answer on the blank line. Use the definitions in the box below to help you.

> A. *a container*
> B. *orange jam*
> C. *where bushes grow*
> D. *a fruit tea or punch*
> E. *a crow or blackbird*
> F. *a painter's color board*

1. _____
2. _____
3. _____
4. _____
5. _____
6. _____

Early humans lived totally off the land. There were no markets at which to shop. They fished and hunted, and they gathered berries from the **1**<u>thicket</u>. They gathered more berries than they could eat, and they stored what was left in a **2**<u>receptacle</u>. Some of the extra berries were used to make a **3**<u>brew</u>. They could not cover their cornbread with **4**<u>marmalade</u>, but they could make a blueberry jam. They also squeezed juice from some of the berries onto a **5**<u>palette</u> for their art projects. The main concern they had was how to protect their supply of berries from the **6**<u>raven</u>.

Directions: Spell each new word three times.

1. thicket _____ _____ _____
2. receptacle _____ _____ _____
3. brew _____ _____ _____
4. marmalade _____ _____ _____
5. palette _____ _____ _____
6. raven _____ _____ _____

Activity: Make a list of your new words in ABC order. Then, write the meaning next to each word.

1. _____ _____
2. _____ _____
3. _____ _____
4. _____ _____
5. _____ _____
6. _____ _____

Enjoy Good Vocabulary!

Directions: Match each idea on the left to an answer on the right. Put the letter of the answer on the blank line. You might need a dictionary to help you.

_____ 1. to laugh sharply

_____ 2. marriage

_____ 3. more than you can count

_____ 4. something that attaches a muscle to a bone

_____ 5. a type of spear

_____ 6. a good place for pigs

_____ 7. a split or separation

_____ 8. a great feeling

_____ 9. a place to sit

_____ 10. to steal the written words of others

_____ 11. a flower that has a pleasant smell

_____ 12. an angry or displeased look

A. tendon

B. cackle

C. sty

D. trident

E. innumerable

F. matrimony

G. jasmine

H. scowl

I. plagiarize

J. stoop

K. rift

L. jubilation

Directions: Spell each new word three times.

1. tendon _____ _____ _____

2. cackle _____ _____ _____

3. sty _____ _____ _____

4. trident _____ _____ _____

5. innumerable _____ _____ _____

6. matrimony _____ _____ _____

7. jasmine _____ _____ _____

8. scowl _____ _____ _____

9. plagiarize _____ _____ _____

10. stoop _____ _____ _____

11. rift _____ _____ _____

12. jubilation _____ _____ _____

Activity: On a separate piece of paper, make four new sentences of your own. Use two new words in each sentence.

Mimi's New Pet

Directions: Find the meaning of each underlined word in the paragraph below. Put the letter of the answer on the blank line. Use the definitions in the box below to help you.

> A. a nice rest
> B. a female cat
> C. a grasshopper
> D. to sweetly love
> E. skillful
> F. a shady place

1. _____
2. _____
3. _____
4. _____
5. _____
6. _____

For Mimi's birthday, her parents gave her a **1**tabby. Her parents had decided that she was mature enough, so now Mimi has her own tabby to **2**cherish. On sunny, summer days Mimi takes her tabby to the front yard. There, the tabby likes to hunt for a **3**katydid. Mimi spreads a blanket under the **4**bower and watches her tabby leap around the yard. Her tabby is very **5**adept at hunting, and soon she has a katydid in her paw. Mimi smiles in her delight and continues her **6**repose under the tree.

Directions: Spell each new word three times.

1. tabby _____ _____ _____
2. cherish _____ _____ _____
3. katydid _____ _____ _____
4. bower _____ _____ _____
5. adept _____ _____ _____
6. repose _____ _____ _____

Activity: Draw a line to connect each idea with the correct new word.

1. able to do well   A. tabby
2. It can have a litter.   B. cherish
3. to have a dear one   C. katydid
4. a break from work   D. bower
5. part of a bug collection E. adept
6. It blocks the sun.   F. repose

The Morning Report

Directions: Read the headlines from the *South Florida Gazette* below. Find the meaning of each underlined word. Put the letter of the answer on the blank line. Use the definitions in the box below to help you.

> A. *to tip and lean to the side*
> B. *handcuffs*
> C. *confusion, commotion*
> D. *to defeat a plan*
> E. *high land near the water*
> F. *a small swamp*

_____ 1. Pilot Spots Eagle's Nest On <u>Promontory</u>

_____ 2. Police <u>Thwart</u> Robber at Supermarket

_____ 3. Overloaded Ships <u>Careen</u> in Gulf Of Mexico

_____ 4. Alligators Caught in <u>Marsh</u> Near Miami

_____ 5. <u>Turmoil</u> at Scene of Local Fire

_____ 6. Sheriff's Department Orders New Supply of <u>Manacles</u>

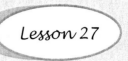

Directions: Spell each new word three times.

1. promontory _____ _____ _____

2. thwart _____ _____ _____

3. careen _____ _____ _____

4. marsh _____ _____ _____

5. turmoil _____ _____ _____

6. manacles _____ _____ _____

Activity: Fill in the blanks with each of your new words.

1. The criminal broke free from his _____.

2. There was _____ at the scene of the train wreck.

3. Too much wind will make the little boat _____ out of control.

4. It is a good view from the _____.

5. He will go bird watching at the edge of the _____.

6. Maybe the principal can _____ the student rebellion.

Good Fun with Words

Directions: Match each idea on the left with the answer to the right. Put the letter of the answer on the blank line. You might need a dictionary to help you.

_____ 1. to pull out a hair or feather	A. tarp
_____ 2. a feeling of emergency	B. chronic
_____ 3. wild and fierce	C. zest
_____ 4. good protection from the weather	D. distress
_____ 5. enthusiasm	E. pluck
_____ 6. persistent, constant	F. ferocious
_____ 7. something nice to sing	G. accessory
_____ 8. move like a butterfly	H. medley
_____ 9. a bunch of rough bushes	I. cadence
_____ 10. something that helps or contributes	J. flit
_____ 11. when a captain loses his power	K. mutiny
_____ 12. a rhythm you can march to	L. chaparral

Directions: Spell each new word three times.

1. tarp _____ _____ _____

2. chronic _____ _____ _____

3. zest _____ _____ _____

4. distress _____ _____ _____

5. pluck _____ _____ _____

6. ferocious _____ _____ _____

7. accessory _____ _____ _____

8. medley _____ _____ _____

9. cadence _____ _____ _____

10. flit _____ _____ _____

11. mutiny _____ _____ _____

12. chaparral _____ _____ _____

Activity: On a separate piece of paper, make four new sentences. Use two of your new words in each sentence.

The Day Is Not Done

Directions: Find the meaning of each underlined word in the schedule below. Put the letter of the answer on the blank line. Use the definitions in the box below to help you.

> A. *nice, polite*
> B. *to solve or understand*
> C. *clothing*
> D. *without mistake*
> E. *to gather up and organize*
> F. *person who is one's equal*

After-School Schedule

_____ 3:30 P.M.—Arrive home and call my <u>peer</u> on the phone

_____ 4:00 P.M.—Spend one hour to <u>cipher</u> my math.

_____ 5:00 P.M.—Have an <u>affable</u> conversation with my mother.

_____ 5:45 P.M.—Begin to <u>compile</u> my notes for my history report.

_____ 7:00 P.M.—Practice my book report out loud. I want it to be <u>impeccable</u>.

_____ 9:00 P.M.—Lay out my <u>garb</u> for school for tomorrow.

Directions: Spell each new word three times.

1. peer _____ _____ _____
2. cipher _____ _____ _____
3. affable _____ _____ _____
4. compile _____ _____ _____
5. impeccable _____ _____ _____
6. garb _____ _____ _____

Activity: Fill in each blank with the best new word.

1. I want to go shopping for new _____ for next summer.

2. She received an A+ for her _____ science project.

3. The governor's son is my _____ at school.

4. I need to _____ all of my papers that are scattered.

5. Did you use a calculator to _____ the algebra problems?

6. I should be _____ even if I am not in a good mood.

Good, Old Computer

Directions: Fill in the missing words in the advertisement below. Use the mini dictionary to help you.

decrepit — broken down
salvage — to save from waste
furnish — to give supplies
tamper — to interfere
assure — to promise
reserve— something saved for future use

Computer For Sale!

This unique machine is a homemade computer that I put together from parts of other computers that I was able to (**1.**) _____. The condition is excellent, and I suggest that you not (**2.**) _____ with it. It will serve you well for many years just as it is. Although it is four years old, it is certainly not (**3.**) _____.

My asking price is $250. That's a good deal, I (**4.**) _____ you! If you have a (**5.**) _____ of money, this would be a good way to spend it. Call me at 555-4120. I will even (**6.**) _____ you with a one-of-a-kind printer that I built from scratch!

Directions: Spell each new word three times.

1. decrepit   _____   _____   _____
2. salvage   _____   _____   _____
3. reserve   _____   _____   _____
4. furnish   _____   _____   _____
5. tamper   _____   _____   _____
6. assure   _____   _____   _____

Activity: Fill in the blanks with your new words.

1. The Abbotts keep a _____ of food in case of an emergency.
2. I can _____ you that my friend can be trusted with your money.
3. The Army will _____ the soldiers with weapons.
4. My washing machine is old and _____ .
5. Do not _____ with my private journal.
6. Could they _____ anything from the shipwreck?

Day or Night, Loose or Tight

Directions: Look at the comparisons. The second description is the opposite of the first. Find the meaning of each underlined word and place the letter of the answer on the blank line. Use the definitions in the box below to help you.

> A. lies, bad tricks
> B. peacefulness
> C. to spend wildly
>
> D. to stare in anger
> E. harmful
> F. shame

_____	1. terrible stress	relaxing <u>tranquility</u>
_____	2. bright with pride	dark with <u>ignominy</u>
_____	3. clean honesty	dirty <u>duplicity</u>
_____	4. greatly helpful	seriously <u>injurious</u>
_____	5. save carefully	<u>squander</u> carelessly
_____	6. to sweetly smile	to hatefully <u>glower</u>

Directions: Spell each new word three times.

1. tranquility _____ _____ _____

2. ignominy _____ _____ _____

3. duplicity _____ _____ _____

4. injurious _____ _____ _____

5. squander _____ _____ _____

6. glower _____ _____ _____

Activity: On a separate piece of paper, use three or four of your new words to write an interesting paragraph. Then complete the following puzzles with your new words.

1. no money left _____

2. a nice rest _____

3. to appear mad _____

4. dishonesty _____

5. not a proud feeling _____

6. not beneficial _____

Night Owls After Midnight

Directions: Answer the riddles below. Write the letter of the vocabulary word on the blank line. Use the mini dictionary to help you.

> A. *ophidian — like a snake*
> B. *ravine — low land area*
> C. *sanctuary — safe shelter*
> D. *stealth — secretive action*
> E. *sylvan — of the forest*
> F. *tuft — a bunch of feathers*

_____ 1. the kind of environment where North American owls live

_____ 2. a place where an owl might spot a rabbit for dinner

_____ 3. where an endangered species of owl might be kept safe

_____ 4. the technique that owls use for their hunting

_____ 5. the covering of an owl's thin legs

_____ 6. describes a creature that is part of an owl's diet

Directions: Spell each new word three times.

1. stealth _____ _____ _____

2. ravine _____ _____ _____

3. tuft _____ _____ _____

4. sylvan _____ _____ _____

5. sanctuary _____ _____ _____

6. ophidian _____ _____ _____

Activity: Complete each of the following analogies with one of your new words.

1. **mountain** is to **valley** as **hill** is to _____

2. **thread** is to **string** as **feather** is to _____

3. **dog** is to **canine** as **snake** is to _____

4. **ice** is to **polar** as **tree** is to _____

5. **house** is to **home** as **zoo** is to _____

6. **teacher** is to **instruction** as **spy** is to _____

Oh, Golly Gee!

Directions: Read the description below of courses offered at a local school. Find each underlined word and place the letter of the answer on the blank line. Use the definitions in the box below to help you.

> A. *courageous*   D. *to grow and develop*
>
> B. *skin tissues*   E. *to reach for a goal*
>
> C. *thickly growing bushes*   F. *rough*

_____ 1. **Geology:** Learn how to polish old and <u>crude</u> rocks, which you find in your own yard.

_____ 2. **Biology:** Observe thin plant and animal <u>membranes</u> under a miscroscope.

_____ 3. **Zoology:** Discover which forest animals live in the <u>underbrush</u>.

_____ 4. **Botany:** Take daily field trips to City Park to observe how plants and grasses <u>flourish</u> in the spring.

_____ 5. **Psychology:** Study the human mind; learn to control your fear and become <u>intrepid</u>.

_____ 6. **Quizology:** If you <u>aspire</u> to get better grades, this course will help you learn to take quizzes.

Directions: Spell each new word three times.

1. crude   _____   _____   _____

2. membranes   _____   _____   _____

3. underbrush   _____   _____   _____

4. flourish   _____   _____   _____

5. intrepid   _____   _____   _____

6. aspire   _____   _____   _____

Activity: Identify each of the following ideas with one of your new words. Write each answer on the blank line provided.

1. Snakes hide here. _____

2. Dream for the best. _____

3. This is certainly not smooth. _____

4. This is another word for "bloom" or "blossom." _____

5. This is one quality of a good soldier. _____

6. These are surface coverings. _____

Capital Pride

Directions: Look below at the list of exciting attractions to be found in Washington, D.C. Find the meaning of each underlined word and put the letter of the answer on the blank line. Use the definitions in the box below to help you.

> A. *large amount*
> B. *convenient and useful*
> C. *a home*
>
> D. *to be respected*
> E. *a vertical structure*
> F. *cannot be compared*

_____ 1. **Washington Monument:** a tall and thin <u>pillar</u>

_____ 2. **Metro:** a swift and <u>expedient</u> underground train

_____ 3. **Capitol Building:** a <u>venerable</u> facility where laws are made

_____ 4. **Smithsonian:** many museums with a <u>plethora</u> of treasures

_____ 5. **Library of Congress:** an <u>incomparable</u> collection of books

_____ 6. **White House:** the <u>abode</u> of the president of the United States

Directions: Spell each new word three times.

1. pillar   _____   _____   _____

2. expedient   _____   _____   _____

3. venerable   _____   _____   _____

4. plethora   _____   _____   _____

5. incomparable _____   _____   _____

6. abode   _____   _____   _____

Activity: Complete the following analogies with your new words.

1. **close** is to **near** as **helpful** is to _____

2. **empty** is to **full** as **nothing** is to _____

3. **bad** is to **good** as **shameful** is to _____

4. **low** is to **stump** as **high** is to _____

5. **animal** is to **barn** as **human** is to _____

6. **same** is to **match** as **different** is to _____

You've Earned It!

Directions: Look over the award below. Find the meaning of each underlined word, and put the letter of the answer on the blank line. Use the definitions in the box below to help you.

A. honorable

B. effort

C. to be guilty of

D. an award

E. a wise person

F. tricky, sneaky

Citizenship Award Winner: Jack Gray, Grade 8

1. _____
2. _____
3. _____
4. _____
5. _____
6. _____

Your principal has selected you as Best Citizen of Stanson Junior High! As a school, we appreciate you and we are happy to give you this **1**merit. Because of your leadership, we trust you would never **2**perpetrate any troubles here or in the community. Your character is honest, and your teachers report no **3**devious actions. You have tried hard, and we recognize your **4**endeavor. Congratulations! Your reputation here is **5**eminent. Keep up your studies, too, and become a **6**savant!

Directions: Spell each new word three times.

1. merit   _____ _____ _____
2. perpetrate   _____ _____ _____
3. devious   _____ _____ _____
4. endeavor   _____ _____ _____
5. eminent   _____ _____ _____
6. savant   _____ _____ _____

Activity: Match each of the following ideas to your new words. Place the letter of the answer in the blank.

_____ 1. a brilliant professor

_____ 2. cannot be trusted

_____ 3. to commit a crime

_____ 4. deserving respect

_____ 5. a great attempt

_____ 6. well-deserved praise

A. devious

B. savant

C. perpetrate

D. endeavor

E. eminent

F. merit

On the African Grasslands

Directions: Use the mini dictionary to help you fill in the missing words in the story below.

treacherous — not to be trusted
humiliation — a loss of pride
deliberate — careful and slow

pelt — animal skin
frayed — ragged and worn out
tawny — yellowish-brown

Many years ago, a native African hunter left his simple, grass hut one morning before dawn. He explained to his wife that he hoped to bring home the (**1.**) _____ of a very old lion that was ready to die. As the native headed out, he immediately saw a (**2.**) _____ shape behind a bush. The native approached the bush cautiously. He knew that even old lions could be (**3.**) _____ . He stood very still, knowing that any movement on his part must be (**4.**) _____ . The native's heart was pounding. He began to raise his spear. Then, looking more closely, he saw that the tawny shape was nothing more than a (**5.**) _____ old blanket. He lowered his great spear in silent (**6.**) _____ .

Directions: Spell each new word three times.

1. treacherous _____ _____ _____

2. humiliation _____ _____ _____

3. deliberate _____ _____ _____

4. pelt _____ _____ _____

5. frayed _____ _____ _____

6. tawny _____ _____ _____

Activity: On a sheet of your own paper, copy the story. Include all of the new words.

In Biology Class

Directions: Find the meaning of each underlined word in the schedule below. Put the letter of the answer on the blank line. Use the definitions in the box below to help you.

> A. *spider web*
> B. *a mineral powder*
> C. *a grassy plant*
> D. *a school of fish*
>
> E. *a large number of something*
> F. *dangerous vapor*
> G. *to twist and squirm*
> H. *to light up*

Unit Highlights for Next Quarter

_____ Week #1: Investigation of <u>talc</u> and other chalk-like substances

_____ Week #2: Field trips to various river banks to study <u>rushes</u>

_____ Week #3: Book research to understand <u>miasma</u> (definitely no field trips)

_____ Week #4: Observations at the zoo (watch snakes <u>writhe</u>)

_____ Week #5: Inspecting a <u>myriad</u> of insect legs

_____ Week #6: Intense study of a black widow's <u>gossamer</u>

_____ Week #7: Research as to how fireflies <u>illuminate</u>

_____ Week #8: Aquarium visit to study a small <u>shoal</u>

Directions: Spell each new word three times.

1. talc _____ _____ _____

2. rushes _____ _____ _____

3. miasma _____ _____ _____

4. writhe _____ _____ _____

5. myriad _____ _____ _____

6. gossamer _____ _____ _____

7. illuminate _____ _____ _____

8. shoal _____ _____ _____

Activity: On a separate piece of paper, make four new sentences. Use at least one word vocabulary word in each.

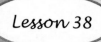

Still a Few Kings

Directions: Find the meaning of each underlined word in the paragraph below. Put the letter of the answer on the blank line. Use the definitions in the box below to help you.

> A. *an admiring respect*
> B. *luxury*
> C. *authority, control*
> D. *an official room*
> E. *to loudly blame*
> F. *healthy*

1. _____
2. _____
3. _____
4. _____
5. _____
6. _____

There are still a few kings in the world. Those kings have **1**<u>dominion</u> over their land and their people. The people of those lands have great respect for their king, and they try to never **2**<u>denounce</u> him. The king spends most of his time in his own **3**<u>chamber</u>, and he lives in great comfort and **4**<u>opulence</u> there. On the rare occasion when he speaks to a crowd, the people treat him with great **5**<u>adulation</u>. They believe he is all-powerful, strong, and **6**<u>hale</u>.

Directions: Spell each new word three times.

1. dominion _____ _____ _____

2. denounce _____ _____ _____

3. chamber _____ _____ _____

4. opulence _____ _____ _____

5. adulation _____ _____ _____

6. hale _____ _____ _____

Activity: Draw a line to connect each phrase to the correct new word.

_____ 1. a very private place   A. hale

_____ 2. not a nice way to announce   B. dominion

_____ 3. in great condition   C. opulence

_____ 4. with great power over others   D. adulation

_____ 5. a warm sense of honor   E. denounce

_____ 6. not a cheap condition   F. chamber

Little Words Mean So Much

Directions: Find the meaning of each underlined word and put the letter of the answer on the blank line.

_____ 1. Wild ducks are in the <u>moor</u>.

_____ 2. He became rich at the <u>lode</u>.

_____ 3. It is too warm for a <u>cloak</u>.

_____ 4. The <u>shaft</u> lit up the sky.

_____ 5. An ant is on the <u>sprig</u>.

_____ 6. The <u>hull</u> needs repair.

_____ 7. Will you <u>buff</u> the silver cup?

_____ 8. See the rabbit on the <u>knoll</u>!

_____ 9. What a terrible <u>stench</u> that is!

_____ 10. The detective <u>foiled</u> the thief's plan.

_____ 11. Poke the potato with the <u>tines</u>.

_____ 12. The horns on a <u>yak</u> are huge.

A. a long, loose coat

B. a ray of lightning

C. land near the water

D. a tiny twig

E. where gold is found

F. the body of a ship

G. a large beast

H. the points of a fork

I. to clean and shine

J. a small hill

K. kept from being successful

L. a very bad smell

Directions: Spell each new word three times.

1. moor _____ _____ _____

2. lode _____ _____ _____

3. cloak _____ _____ _____

4. shaft _____ _____ _____

5. sprig _____ _____ _____

6. hull _____ _____ _____

7. buff _____ _____ _____

8. knoll _____ _____ _____

9. stench _____ _____ _____

10. foiled _____ _____ _____

11. tines _____ _____ _____

12. yak _____ _____ _____

Activity: On a separate piece of paper, make three new sentences of your own. Use at least two new words in each sentence.

A Rescue at the Lake

Directions: Find the meaning of each underlined word in the newspaper article below. Put the letter of the answer on the blank line. Use the definitions in the box below to help you.

> A. a very wild action
> B. a feeling of regret
> C. advantage, worth
> D. to give up, to be overwhelmed
> E. scorching, hot
> F. error

Near Disaster at Local Lake

1. _____
2. _____
3. _____
4. _____
5. _____
6. _____

Two teen-aged boys nearly drowned last Sunday at Lake Wilson. It had been a [1]torrid day, with a high of 98 degrees. The boys were paddling a canoe, when they jumped overboard to take a swim. It was nearly a costly mistake. The boys were not good swimmers, and they quickly became fearful. The boys screamed for help, but it seemed to be to no [2]avail. They became desperate and had deep [3]remorse for their mistake. Their actions became a [4]frenzy to survive. Just as the boys were about to [5]succumb, a county lifeguard reached them with two life rings. The saved boys did not need to be told twice that their decision to leave the canoe had been a horrible [6]blunder.

Directions: Spell each new word three times.

1. torrid _____ _____ _____
2. avail _____ _____ _____
3. remorse _____ _____ _____
4. frenzy _____ _____ _____
5. succumb _____ _____ _____
6. blunder _____ _____ _____

Activity: Circle the best answer for each idea.

1. not a calm situation   **torrid** or **frenzy**
2. a sorry feeling   **remorse** or **avail**
3. like summer in Hawaii   **frenzy** or **torrid**
4. to use an opportunity   **blunder** or **avail**
5. to give up the life breath   **succumb** or **remorse**
6. a big goof-up   **torrid** or **blunder**

Rainy Day Journal Notes

Directions: Find the meaning of each underlined word in the paragraph below. Put the letter of the answer on the blank line. Use the definitions in the box below to help you.

> A. *many, various*
> B. *jolly*
> C. *to wish or dream*
> D. *to change or transform*
> E. *not satisfied*
> F. *a person's face*

1. _____
2. _____
3. _____
4. _____
5. _____
6. _____

Some people feel sad or gloomy on a rainy day, but I feel absolutely **1**jovial. Perhaps the reason I enjoy the rain is that my imagination runs wild, and I think of **2**sundry things to do. I cook, I read, I even clean out my closet! I paint, I draw, I even organize my notebook. On a rainy day, I do not sit and **3**yearn for sunshine. I love the rain! I think the rain **4**transfigures the world into a more beautiful place. Rain never makes me **5**discontent. It excites me and gives me energy! In fact, the rain lights up my whole **6**visage.

Directions: Spell each new word three times.

1. jovial   _____ _____ _____

2. sundry   _____ _____ _____

3. yearn   _____ _____ _____

4. transfigures _____ _____ _____

5. discontent _____ _____ _____

6. visage   _____ _____ _____

Activity: Put your new words into ABC order. Next to each word, write its meaning.

1. _____   _____
2. _____   _____
3. _____   _____
4. _____   _____
5. _____   _____
6. _____   _____

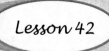

Lost Animal Alert

Directions: Find the meaning of each underlined word and put the letter of the answer on the blank line. Use the definitions in the box below to help you.

> A. *wild cherries*
> B. *with blooming flowers*
> C. *a donkey's sound*
> D. *silly, foolish*
> E. *a shine*
> F. *wing feathers*

_____ 1. Lost: Beautiful yellow bird with some missing <u>pinions</u>.

_____ 2. Lost: Listen for the <u>bray</u> of this missing animal.

_____ 3. Lost: Large pet turtle with a nice <u>luster</u> on its shell.

_____ 4. Lost: Zoo's baby bear — He might be in the forest nibbling on <u>marascas</u>.

_____ 5. Lost: Family's pet butterfly — Please check all <u>floriferous</u> areas.

_____ 6. Lost: Little kitten who has many <u>fatuous</u> actions.

Directions: Spell each new word three times.

1. pinions _____ _____ _____

2. bray _____ _____ _____

3. luster _____ _____ _____

4. marascas _____ _____ _____

5. floriferous _____ _____ _____

6. fatuous _____ _____ _____

Activity: Draw a line to connect each idea to the best new word.

1. without much serious thought

2. writing tools, perhaps

3. could make a nice pie filling

4. something you might hear on a farm

5. a pretty area in the springtime

6. increased by polishing

A. pinions

B. luster

C. fatuous

D. floriferous

E. bray

F. marascas

News from the Zoo

Directions: Use the mini dictionary to help you fill in the missing words in the story below.

> wallow — to roll in mud
> inception — beginning
> critters — creatures
>
> colossal — huge
> mustang — a wild horse
> confound — to confuse

The Zoo of Friendly Living has announced major changes to some of its attractions. Please pick up the information sheet at the zoo's entrance so that the changes will not (**1.**) _____ you. The zoo has expanded the grasslands, so that its prized (**2.**) _____ may gallop. More dirt and water have been added for the wild pigs to (**3.**) _____ . Workers have finished building a (**4.**) _____ tower on which the eagles can build their nests, and little cages have been built for the smaller (**5.**) _____ , as well. All of these changes mark the (**6.**) _____ of the zoo's new image.

Directions: Spell each new word three times.

1. wallow _____ _____ _____

2. inception _____ _____ _____

3. critters _____ _____ _____

4. colossal _____ _____ _____

5. mustang _____ _____ _____

6. confound _____ _____ _____

Activity: Circle the best new word to match each idea.

1. to create something unclear **colossal** or **confound**

2. dirty and messy **mustang** or **wallow**

3. a cowboy could tame it **inception** or **mustang**

4. not tiny at all **colossal** or **wallow**

5. the start of a new plan **inception** or **critters**

6. they're everywhere **confound** or **critters**

Community Carnival

Directions: Find the meaning of each underlined word below. Put the letter of the answer on the blank line. Use the definitions in the box below to help you.

> A. cheap toys
>
> B. a tricky person
>
> C. main character
>
> D. to run hard
>
> E. a location
>
> F. a large dog

Carnival Coming to Town!

May 15–17 @ 4:00 P.M.

1. _____

2. _____

3. _____

4. _____

5. _____

6. _____

Where: Daisy Park will be the **1**<u>venue</u>.

Come get your corn dogs, cotton candy, and dill pickles! You can **2**<u>sprint</u> for cash prizes, and win **3**<u>trinkets</u> at the ball toss. There will be balloons, flags, and pinwheels. Soda, cider, and lemonade will be served! Win big if you guess the correct weight of Smokey the **4**<u>mastiff</u>. Take part in a comedy skit, with you as the **5**<u>protagonist</u>!

Bring your nickels, dimes, and quarters! But play wisely and try to outsmart the **6**<u>knave</u>! He is out to get your hard-earned money.

Directions: Spell each new word three times.

1. venue   _____   _____   _____

2. sprint   _____   _____   _____

3. trinkets   _____   _____   _____

4. mastiff   _____   _____   _____

5. protagonist   _____   _____   _____

6. knave   _____   _____   _____

Activity: Fill in the blanks with your own words.

1. I would not play card games with a _____.

2. Did you buy any _____ when you were on vacation?

3. Where is the _____ for the birthday party?

4. I would choose a poodle puppy, not a _____.

5. We had to _____ in P.E. yesterday.

6. The _____ of the story was not evil.

A Peak Experience

Directions: Find the meaning of each underlined word in the letter below. Put the letter of the answer on the blank line. Use the definitions in the box below to help you.

A. *highest point*
B. *sudden rush*
C. *clumsy, not smooth*
D. *doubtful*
E. *a dangerous cliff*
F. *mental determination*

Dear Adventurers,

1. _____

2. _____

3. _____

4. _____

5. _____

6. _____

I am happy you have joined my team to climb Mount Block. I hope each of you is really ready. You will need a strong **1**<u>resolve</u> to accomplish this! Now, trust in yourself: it is risky to climb if your mind is **2**<u>dubious</u>.

Safety is very important to me. I assure you that we will encounter more than one steep **3**<u>crag</u>. An **4**<u>ungainly</u> person would have no business attempting this climb. But for those of us who can, we will feel the **5**<u>surge</u> of excitement as we near the top. And when we reach the **6**<u>apex</u>, you will see that the whole trip was worth everything you have put into it!

Directions: Spell each new word three times.

1. resolve _____ _____ _____

2. dubious _____ _____ _____

3. crag _____ _____ _____

4. ungainly _____ _____ _____

5. surge _____ _____ _____

6. apex _____ _____ _____

Activity: Identify each idea with the best new word. Write the answer on the blank line.

1. not graceful _____

2. a quick, new power _____

3. my own promise _____

4. very rough edge _____

5. the peak _____

6. feeling unsure _____

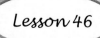

The Cabin

Directions: Find the meaning of each underlined word in the paragraph below. Put the letter of the answer on the blank line. Use the definitions in the box below to help you.

> A. *cracked openings*   D. *to bring back to use*
>
> B. *high, flat land*   E. *wooden boards*
>
> C. *a lot of something*   F. *an ax*

1. _____
2. _____
3. _____
4. _____
5. _____
6. _____

Grandfather has a very old cabin near the river. It is not on the shore; it is on a **¹**plateau where he can look down on the river below. He has decided to fix up his old cabin. He is nailing new **²**planks to the floor. He is putting more mud into the **³**chinks between the fireplace bricks. He will chop up old roots and bushes with his **⁴**mattock and plant a nice flower garden. He wants to grow **⁵**scads of yellow daisies there. He thinks that if he can **⁶**revive the old cabin, he will spend more time there.

Directions: Spell each new word three times.

1. plateau   _____   _____   _____

2. planks   _____   _____   _____

3. chinks   _____   _____   _____

4. mattock   _____   _____   _____

5. scads   _____   _____   _____

6. revive   _____   _____   _____

Activity: Match each idea to the correct new word. Put the letter of the answer on the blank line.

_____ 1. plateau   A. It is sharp.

_____ 2. planks   B. It is more than enough.

_____ 3. chinks   C. They are for building.

_____ 4. mattock   D. This is like bringing something back to life

_____ 5. scads   E. Spiders could hide here.

_____ 6. revive   F. There's a good view from here.

See You Next Summer

Directions: Use the mini dictionary to help you fill in the missing words in the letter below.

> *downhearted — sad*
> *requisite — necessary*
> *defunct — done, at the end*
>
> *courier — a messenger*
> *valiant — brave*
> *yearn — to strongly wish for*

Dear Maria,

Moving away has been hard for me. I already miss you so much. I know I will see you in July, but I (**1.**) _____ to see you before that. You are my best friend. Did you know that?

Mom knows that I have been feeling (**2.**) _____ about moving away. She gave me a pretty bracelet to cheer me up. She told me there are always many changes in life, and a person must remain (**3.**) _____.

I will try to make new friends soon. I know that a friendly smile is (**4.**) _____ for that. Just remember—our own friendship will never be (**5.**) _____.

I am sending this letter by (**6.**) _____. I hope it arrives safely.

Love,

Julia

Directions: Spell each new word three times.

1. downhearted _____ _____ _____
2. requisite _____ _____ _____
3. defunct _____ _____ _____
4. courier _____ _____ _____
5. valiant _____ _____ _____
6. yearn _____ _____ _____

Activity: On a sheet of your own paper, rewrite the letter above with the missing words filled in.

A Riddle to Fiddle About

Directions: Read each riddle below and find the underlined words. Use the definitions in the box below to help you. How many of these riddles can you answer?

> A. *a pretty girl*
> B. *a long story*
> C. *a bunch of noises*
> D. *blurry, fuzzy*
> E. *held back by delays*
> F. *shocked, expressing disbelief*

_____ 1. Crowds of people everywhere made a <u>din</u> when gold was discovered in 1849 in this state.

_____ 2. An American spy plane made an emergency landing in this country in 2001 and was <u>detained</u> there for two weeks.

_____ 3. This <u>nebulous</u> area in space contains our own solar system.

_____ 4. You might have heard a <u>saga</u> about the buffalo that still roam around this national park.

_____ 5. A beast falls in love with a <u>belle</u> in this famous animated film.

_____ 6. The public had an <u>incredulous</u> reaction when this man's invention of the telephone really worked!

Directions: Spell each new word three times.

1. din _____ _____ _____

2. detained _____ _____ _____

3. nebulous _____ _____ _____

4. saga _____ _____ _____

5. belle _____ _____ _____

6. incredulous _____ _____ _____

Activity: Complete each sentence with one of your new words.

1. That elderly movie star was a _____ when she was young.

2. Did your grandmother ever tell you a _____ about her childhood?

3. The man was _____ when he learned that his car had been stolen.

4. The teacher was frustrated when she could not quiet the _____ in her classroom

5. The film's plot was _____ and difficult to understand.

6. The police _____ several people for questioning.

Desert Blooms

Directions: Read the following field-trip permission slip. Find the meaning of each underlined word, and place the letter of its meaning on the blank line. Use the definitions in the box below to help you.

> A. fascinating
> B. boring
> C. to start out
>
> D. aware
> E. brief, quick
> F. to outline a sketch

Permission Slip

1. _____

2. _____

3. _____

4. _____

5. _____

6. _____

Our class will be planning to **¹embark** on a field trip to the desert on April 28th. Many people think that the desert is a colorless and **²humdrum** place. Actually, springtime in the desert can be very **³captivating**!

When we arrive, students will immediately become **⁴cognizant** of new life as they spot colorful flower blossoms everywhere! And these blossoms must be enjoyed now because in a **⁵fleeting** time, they will be gone.

When we return from our desert travels, I will ask each student to **⁶delineate** a desert scene.

Directions: Spell each new word three times.

1. embark _____ _____ _____

2. humdrum _____ _____ _____

3. captivating _____ _____ _____

4. cognizant _____ _____ _____

5. fleeting _____ _____ _____

6. delineate _____ _____ _____

Activity: Complete the following analogies with your new words.

1. **come back** is to **return** as **go** is to _____

2. **long** is to **continuing** as **short** is to _____

3. **fun** is to **interesting** as **dull** is to _____

4. **brush** is to **paint** as **pencil** is to _____

5. **awful** is to **wonderful** as **dull** is to _____

6. **dull** is to **alert** as **asleep** is to _____

Cafeteria Cookin'

Directions: Find the meaning of each underlined word in the school lunch menu below. Put the letter of the answer on the blank line. Use the definitions in the box below to help you.

> A. *to make a temptation*
> B. *small cucumbers*
> C. *a barrel*
>
> D. *hot, boiled corn*
> E. *strongly flavorful*
> F. *meat from a sheep*

Today's Lunch

_____ 1. steaming bowl of <u>hominy</u> (North American style) — $1.00

_____ 2. plate of beef with <u>pungent</u> onions — $2.00

_____ 3. salad with tomatoes and <u>gherkins</u> — $1.00

_____ 4. baked lamb (not <u>mutton</u>) — $2.00

_____ 5. delicious apple cider from a wooden <u>cask</u> — $1.00

_____ 6. ice cream with hot fudge to <u>tantalize</u> you —$1.00

Directions: Spell each new word three times.

1. hominy _____ _____ _____

2. pungent _____ _____ _____

3. gherkins _____ _____ _____

4. mutton _____ _____ _____

5. cask _____ _____ _____

6. tantalize _____ _____ _____

Activity: Complete the following analogies using your new words.

1. **fruit** is to **orange** as **vegetable** is to _____

2. **book** is to **shelf** as **water** is to _____

3. **feel** is to **soft** as **taste** is to _____

4. **raisins** are to **grapes** as **pickles** are to _____

5. **noun** is to **table** as **verb** is to _____

6. **grain** is to **wheat** as **meat** is to _____

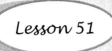

Above the Land

Directions: Find the meaning of each underlined word in the paragraph below. Put the letter of the answer on the blank line. Use the definitions in the box below to help you.

> A. high in the air   D. a type of hawk
>
> B. unlucky   E. insufficient
>
> C. tiny rivers   F. fierce character

1. _____
2. _____
3. _____
4. _____
5. _____
6. _____

A creature that spends most of its day high above the land is the **1**osprey. It takes advantage of its **2**aerial life when hunting for food. From the sky, it watches for fish down below in the lakes and the **3**rills. The **4**hapless fish are quickly spotted by the sharp-eyed osprey. The **5**ferocity of the osprey gives the fish no chance to escape. The osprey then enjoys more than a **6**meager lunch!

Directions: Spell each new word three times.

1. osprey   _____ _____ _____

2. aerial   _____ _____ _____

3. rills   _____ _____ _____

4. hapless   _____ _____ _____

5. ferocity   _____ _____ _____

6. meager   _____ _____ _____

Activity: Identify each idea with the best new word. Write the answer on the blank line.

1. without good fortune   _____

2. a swift and strong creature   _____

3. not kindness   _____

4. a flyer's position   _____

5. a place to splash   _____

6. poor in money or supply   _____

New at the Theaters

Directions: Find the meaning of each underlined word in the paragraph below. Put the letter of the answer on the blank line. Use the definitions in the box below to help you.

> A. draw back from danger
> B. standing position
> C. steal
> D. a brief battle
> E. be interesting
> F. a pirate

1. _____
2. _____
3. _____
4. _____
5. _____
6. _____

A famous producer has just released his newest movie. It is an adventurous story of a wild ¹buccaneer in the year 1738. The title of the movie is *Many a* ²*Skirmish at Sea*, and there is enough action in it to make anyone ³flinch. This movie will ⁴appeal to people of all ages who enjoy a fast-paced story. The wild buccaneer overpowers one ship after another to ⁵plunder from them. On the deck of his own ship, he takes a ⁶stance that even his own crew members fear.

Directions: Spell each new word three times.

1. buccaneer _____ _____ _____

2. skirmish _____ _____ _____

3. flinch _____ _____ _____

4. appeal _____ _____ _____

5. plunder _____ _____ _____

6. stance _____ _____ _____

Activity: Complete each sentence with one new word.

1. It is against the law to destroy or _____ other people's property.

2. Which actor plays the part of the _____ in the new movie?

3. Two small armies had a _____ at the top of the hill.

4. If you want to be a good hitter in baseball, your _____ is very important.

5. A batter who is afraid of getting hit might _____ when pitched to.

6. Does a visit to the zoo _____ to you?

Figure It Out!

Directions: Use the mini dictionary to help you answer the riddles below.

> A. *bangle* — *a bracelet*
> B. *bounty* — *reward money*
> C. *conflagration* — *a large fire*
> D. *flotsam* — *stuff from a shipwreck*
> E. *apparition* — *a ghost*
> F. *chard* — *a leafy vegetable*
> G. *chronicle* — *a record of history*
> H. *blemish* — *a spot or stain*

_____ 1. This might be earned for a finding a missing pet.

_____ 2. This provides great vitamins.

_____ 3. This makes something less than perfect.

_____ 4. This would make a very nice present.

_____ 5. This has many important dates and years.

_____ 6. This would give anyone a scare.

_____ 7. This would float on the surface.

_____ 8. This would cause a lot of destruction.

Directions: Spell each new word three times.

1. bangle _____ _____ _____

2. bounty _____ _____ _____

3. conflagration _____ _____ _____

4. flotsam _____ _____ _____

5. apparition _____ _____ _____

6. chard _____ _____ _____

7. chronicle _____ _____ _____

8. blemish _____ _____ _____

Activity: Fill in the blank with the new word that fits best.

1. The newspaper gave a complete _____ of the mayor's political career.

2. She wrapped the silver _____ in tissue and put it in a small box.

3. A parking ticket was the only _____ on her driving record.

4. She was busy chopping the _____ for her famous soup.

5. The story's main character is an _____ who haunts an old mansion.

6. How much of a _____ will they pay for information?

7. A crew will need to clean up the _____ along the island's shore.

8. The _____ destroyed a large pine forest outside of town.

To Mars and Back

Directions: Find the meaning of each underlined word in the paragraph below. Put the letter of the answer on the blank line. Use the definitions in the box below to help you.

> A. excited interest
> B. complicated
> C. to supply
> D. a disbeliever
> E. lacking in amount
> F. with a lot of luxury

1. _____

2. _____

3. _____

4. _____

5. _____

6. _____

It won't be long before astronauts will be heading for Mars. NASA is currently working out many [1]intricate details for a round-trip journey. Scientists are filled with [2]ardor about these plans. Hour by hour, they discuss how to make a successful journey to Mars. One serious point of discussion is how to [3]purvey enough food and water for the mission. Supplies must not be [4]deficient. The trip will certainly not be [5]opulent, but there must be enough supplies for survival. Anyone who is a [6]skeptic should not apply for the mission to Mars.

Directions: Spell each new word three times.

1. intricate _____ _____ _____

2. ardor _____ _____ _____

3. purvey _____ _____ _____

4. deficient _____ _____ _____

5. opulent _____ _____ _____

6. skeptic _____ _____ _____

Activity: First, put all of your new words in ABC order. Beside each new word, write its meaning.

1. _____ _____

2. _____ _____

3. _____ _____

4. _____ _____

5. _____ _____

6. _____ _____

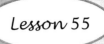

Marvelous Mysteries

Directions: Find the meaning of each underlined word and put the letter of the answer on the blank line. Use the definitions in the box below to help you.

> A. *a very independent person*   D. *an illness*
> B. *something that threatens*   E. *a kind of seashell*
> C. *to raid*   F. *a design theme*

_____ 1. Why do so many humans consider a spider to be a <u>menace</u>?

_____ 2. Why do most old people suffer from a <u>malady</u> or two?

_____ 3. Why was a <u>maverick</u> the image of the American cowboy?

_____ 4. Why do little ants always seem to <u>maraud</u> our picnics?

_____ 5. What type of snail lives inside a <u>murex</u>?

_____ 6. How did the weaver ever create such an intricate <u>motif</u>?

Directions: Spell each new word three times.

1. menace   _____ _____ _____

2. malady   _____ _____ _____

3. maverick   _____ _____ _____

4. maraud   _____ _____ _____

5. murex   _____ _____ _____

6. motif   _____ _____ _____

Activity: Fill in each blank with the new word that fits best.

1. He searched the beach for the _____ he needed to complete his collection.

2. They say he is a _____ because he left his hometown for Mexico.

3. She bought wallpaper that had a flowery _____.

4. A poisonous snake is certainly a _____ to those who cross its path.

5. He is in the hospital because of a serious _____.

6. Pirates were known to _____ passing ships.

Plenty of Work, Plenty of Play

Directions: Study the weekly planner below. Use the mini dictionary to fill in each missing word.

> *sappy — silly, foolish*
> *scrupulous — careful, exact*
> *clarity — clearness*
> *perplex — to confuse*
> *perusal — a careful study*
> *omniscient — having total knowledge*

MON — Prepare a (**1.**) _____ science chart by using a ruler.

TUES — Make a (**2.**) _____ of this week's spelling words and try for 100% on the test.

WED — Spend two hours on the computer to research my project, but don't expect the computer to be (**3.**) _____ .

THURS — Practice my magic trick several times for tomorrow's party. I want to (**4.**) _____ everyone!

FRI — The week is over! Take a long shower and go to the party.

SAT — Enjoy a totally (**5.**) _____ comedy. Don't think too much!

SUN — Practice my speech for history class out loud several times so I will be ready to speak with perfect (**6.**) _____ .

Directions: Spell each new word three times.

1. sappy
2. scrupulous
3. clarity
4. perplex
5. perusal
6. omniscient

Activity: Draw a line to connect each of the following ideas to the correct answer.

1. Nobody is this perfect.
2. An accountant should be like this.
3. A good public speaker needs this.
4. This is a complete review.
5. A clown might be this way.
6. To cause a mix-up in the mind.

A. omniscient
B. perusal
C. scrupulous
D. perplex
E. clarity
F. sappy

Girls' and Guys' Disguises

Directions: Read the ads below. Use the mini dictionary to help you fill in the missing words.

> *hideous – horrible*
> *statesman – a public leader*
> *firelock – an early rifle*
> *phantasm – a ghostly presence*
> *baron – a king's nobleman*
> *insignia – a symbol*

HALLOWEEN RENTALS (*only $9.99 each!*)

1. Wear an Official Dark Suit and Tie, Be a _____!

2. A Simple White Sheet Will Turn You Into a Spooky _____!

3. Get Your Superman's Cape With the Traditional _____ On the Front!

4. This _____ Monster Costume Will Make Everyone You Encounter Scream!

5. Get an Authentic Davy Crocket Costume (Even Includes a Toy _____)!

6. With These Toy Jewels and Velvet Robe, You'll Be Dressed Like a _____!

Directions: Spell each new word three times.

1. hideous   _____   _____   _____

2. statesman   _____   _____   _____

3. firelock   _____   _____   _____

4. phantasm   _____   _____   _____

5. baron   _____   _____   _____

6. insignia   _____   _____   _____

Activity: Draw a line to connect each of the following ideas to the correct new word.

1. a senator perhaps   A. baron

2. used by pioneers   B. phantasm

3. one who might bow royally   C. hideous

4. a company logo   D. insignia

5. spooky image   E. statesman

6. super awful   F. firelock

Reward Money Offered

Directions: Use the mini dictionary to help you fill in the missing words in the story below.

diffident — shy	*defray — to pay the cost*
bog — swamp, marsh	*revel — to celebrate*
plumage — set of feathers	*ploy — a clever trick*

PLEASE HELP!!! Two days ago my pet parrot escaped. I opened his cage to clean it, and he flew out my front door! I will pay $55.00 for my parrot's return. His (1.) _____ is bright, but his character is (2.) _____ . He might be headed towards the (3.) _____ to hang out with the ducks. If you spot him, please use any (4.) _____ to capture him. I will (5.) _____ the cost of any treats that you use to bring him back to me. Please! If you find my parrot, then we can all (6.) _____ .

Directions: Spell each new word three times.

1. diffident _____ _____ _____

2. bog _____ _____ _____

3. plumage _____ _____ _____

4. defray _____ _____ _____

5. revel _____ _____ _____

6. ploy _____ _____ _____

Activity: First, put all of your new words in ABC order below. Next to each word, write its definition.

1. _____ _____

2. _____ _____

3. _____ _____

4. _____ _____

5. _____ _____

6. _____ _____

Use Your Brain Power

Directions: Use the mini dictionary to help you answer the riddles below.

> *tribulation — a lot of great troubles*
> *premiere — the first performance*
> *bunker — an underground shelter*
> *correspondent — a reporter sent to a faraway place*
>
> *cavalcade — a group of horse riders*
> *testimony — a statement of facts*
> *toupee — a man's wig*
> *despot — a ruler with absolute power*

1. I am what the audience is waiting for. _____
2. I am someone the people might fear. _____
3. I am sometimes a part of a parade. _____
4. I am a challenge to your patience and courage. _____
5. I could be a part of a costume. _____
6. I can be a soldier's defense. _____
7. I am the words from a witness to a crime. _____
8. I relay current information. _____

Directions: Spell each new word three times.

1. tribulation _____ _____ _____
2. premiere _____ _____ _____
3. bunker _____ _____ _____
4. correspondent _____ _____ _____
5. cavalcade _____ _____ _____
6. testimony _____ _____ _____
7. toupee _____ _____ _____
8. despot _____ _____ _____

Activity: Fill in each sentence with the best new word.

1. The group planned a revolution to overthrow the _____.
2. He escaped injury by crawling into a _____.
3. The tickets for the play's _____ were quite expensive.
4. Grampa doesn't allow anyone to play with the _____ on his head.
5. Much of the _____ in the world is caused by wars.
6. The sight of the _____ entertained the crowd.
7. She is based in London as a television _____.
8. It is illegal to lie during _____ in a court of law.

Space Station 2009

Directions: Find the meaning of each underlined word in the paragraph below. Put the letter of the answer on the blank line. Use the definitions in the box below to help you.

> A. *majestic, grand*
> B. *extremely forceful*
> C. *public notice*
> D. *conquer, overcome*
> E. *to use a supply*
> F. *restless, nervous*

1. _____ Astronaut: "The views we are getting from our space station back to Earth are truly **1**<u>sublime</u>! In fact, with views like this, we are in no hurry to finish our mission."

2. _____ Ground Control: "Then you won't be disappointed with what we have to tell you. Our computers are giving us trouble, and there are technical problems to **2**<u>surmount</u> before we can bring you home."

3. _____ Astronaut: "Well, everyone is jolly and healthy up here. So, take your time to fix whatever is wrong. There's no need to do anything **3**<u>drastic</u>."

Ground Control: "We don't want the news media to give our problems any
4. _____ **4**<u>publicity</u> so it's just between you up there and us down here."

Astronaut: "As I've said, we are happy here for the moment, and our work is going well. We are all calm and satisfied with our mission. If any crew
5. _____ members become **5**<u>restive</u>, I will let you know."

Ground Control: "Then, let your experiments go for a few more days. Film as much of your work as you can. Drink plenty of fluids, and don't
6. _____ **6**<u>consume</u> too many snacks."

Directions: Spell each new word three times.

1. sublime _____ _____ _____

2. surmount _____ _____ _____

3. drastic _____ _____ _____

4. publicity _____ _____ _____

5. restive _____ _____ _____

6. consume _____ _____ _____

Activity: On a separate piece of paper, create two sentences of your own. Use two new words in each sentence.

Out of Cash

Directions: Look at the advertisement below. Find the meaning of each underlined word and put the letter of the answer on the blank line. Use the definitions in the box below to help you.

> A. *to be trusted*
> B. *without error*
> C. *very important*
> D. *a sheep*
> E. *a deep kindness*
> F. *not fresh and bright*

Work Needed! High school girl will do odd jobs for pocket money! Available after school and weekends. Call Tiffany at 555-2030. Here are my strengths:

_____ 1. If you need a typist, call me. My typing work is clean and <u>unblemished</u>!

_____ 2. If you need a babysitter, I enjoy young children and have <u>solicitude</u> for them.

_____ 3. If you have private papers to organize, my work is <u>confidential</u>.

_____ 4. If you need someone to take care of your <u>shearling</u>, I grew up on a farm and can help you!

_____ 5. If you have a <u>memorable</u> day to celebrate, I can help you plan a party!

_____ 6. If your office is looking <u>dingy</u> these days, I can help you paint it.

Directions: Spell each new word three times.

1. unblemished _____ _____ _____

2. solicitude _____ _____ _____

3. confidential _____ _____ _____

4. shearling _____ _____ _____

5. memorable _____ _____ _____

6. dingy _____ _____ _____

Activity: Fill in the blanks below with your new words.

1. A good nurse should have a natural _____ toward her patients.

2. Winning first prize in the poetry contest was a _____ event for me.

3. Please keep the information that I tell you _____ .

4. We stayed in an old motel that was very _____ .

5. Paul was given extra credit for his _____ attendance record.

6. The biology class studied everything from a butterfly to a _____ .

The Pool Will Open

Directions: Use the mini dictionary to help you fill in the story below.

> fliers — news bulletins
> adhere — to stick to
> diligent — hard-working
>
> unruly — badly behaved
> unfurl — to unfold and spread out
> paramount — supreme, main

The community pool will open for the summer on May 15th! The lifeguard staff will
(**1.**) _____ a long flag to hang at the gate. They will also be passing out
(**2.**) _____ in the neighborhood to announce the pool's opening. The
lifeguards have been training all spring for their duty. Swimmers' safety will be their
(**3.**) _____ concern. Everyone is expected to (**4.**) _____
to the rules. The lifeguards will be very (**5.**) _____ when they are on
duty, and they expect everyone's cooperation. Any (**6.**) _____ children
will be asked to leave the pool.

Directions: Spell each new word three times.

1. fliers _____ _____ _____

2. adhere _____ _____ _____

3. diligent _____ _____ _____

4. unruly _____ _____ _____

5. unfurl _____ _____ _____

6. paramount _____ _____ _____

Activity: Circle the best answer to each question.

1. Which would be printed on paper? **paramount** or **fliers**

2. What will a stamp do? **unfurl** or **adhere**

3. Which word will keep you out of trouble? **unruly** or **diligent**

4. Which word indicates the very top? **paramount** or **adhere**

5. What will a curled up leaf do? **unfurl** or **unruly**

6. Which one needs correction? **diligent** or **unruly**

The Morning Headlines

Directions: Look at each newspaper headline below. Find the meaning of each underlined word and put the letter of the answer on the blank line.

_____	1. <u>Verdict</u> Announced in Thief's Trial	A. a deep crack
_____	2. City Zoo Displays <u>Behemoth</u>	B. making a profit
_____	3. Community Says Garbage Dump Is <u>Putrid</u>	C. a court decision
_____	4. New Local Business Very <u>Lucrative</u>	D. one who is masterful (often a musician)
_____	5. Earthquake in Alaska Creates <u>Chasm</u>	E. something huge (often an animal)
_____	6. <u>Virtuoso</u> Performs This Friday	F. terribly smelly
_____	7. <u>Ingenious</u> New Bicycle On the Market	G. cleverly invented
_____	8. Bank Robber <u>Evades</u> Police	H. tries to escape
_____	9. Florida Park Filled with <u>Palmettos</u>	I. to make less severe
_____	10. <u>Premonition</u> of Fire Saves Family	J. to spread out soldiers
_____	11. Army General Will <u>Deploy</u> Troops	K. small palm trees
_____	12. New Medicine to <u>Mitigate</u> Pain	L. a feeling of danger

Directions: Spell each new word three times.

1. verdict _____ _____ _____

2. behemoth _____ _____ _____

3. putrid _____ _____ _____

4. lucrative _____ _____ _____

5. chasm _____ _____ _____

6. virtuoso _____ _____ _____

7. ingenious _____ _____ _____

8. evade _____ _____ _____

9. palmetto _____ _____ _____

10. premonition _____ _____ _____

11. deploy _____ _____ _____

12. mitigate _____ _____ _____

Activity: On a separate piece of paper, make three new sentences of your own by using two new words in each sentence.

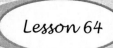

Caught in a Snowstorm

Directions: Find the meaning of each underlined word in the paragraph below. Put the letter of the answer on the blank line. Use the definitions in the box below to help you.

> A. very hungry
> B. used a supply
> C. very carefully
> D. a small journey
> E. to speed up
> F. flowing together

1. _____
2. _____
3. _____
4. _____
5. _____
6. _____

An early snowstorm caught two hikers unprepared yesterday. The hikers had left town at dawn on a simple ¹excursion. They had planned to follow the river to the point of the three ²confluent streams. They had reached that point and begun their return when heavy snow began falling. They could not ³accelerate their pace without slipping and sliding. So, instead of trying to hurry home, they began to step ⁴gingerly. A four-hour hike turned into an eight-hour excursion. They were ⁵famished when they finally reached town. They had ⁶depleted the few snacks they carried with them.

Directions: Spell each new word three times.

1. excursion _____ _____ _____
2. confluent _____ _____ _____
3. accelerate _____ _____ _____
4. gingerly _____ _____ _____
5. famished _____ _____ _____
6. depleted _____ _____ _____

Activity: Draw a line to connect each idea with the best new word.

1. needing to eat   A. depleted
2. a little trip   B. gingerly
3. all used up   C. famished
4. not carelessly   D. excursion
5. joining together   E. accelerate
6. to gain or increase   F. confluent

Consider This Lunch

Directions: Find the meaning of each underlined word on the school menu below. Put the letter of the answer on the blank line. Use the definitions in the box below to help you.

> A. *a flavorful decoration*   D. *chicken or turkey*
>
> B. *to enjoy the flavor*   E. *beans or peas*
>
> C. *a place where bees are kept* F. *peanuts*

School Lunch Menu — Wednesday, March 6

_____ 1. Choice of ham or a piece of <u>poultry</u>

_____ 2. Muffin with honey delivered fresh from the <u>apiary</u>

_____ 3. A cup of soup with carrots and <u>legumes</u>

_____ 4. A handful of crunchy <u>goobers</u>

_____ 5. Milk or juice to <u>savor</u> with your meal

_____ 6. A cupcake with a frosting <u>garnish</u> on top

Directions: Spell each new word three times.

1. poultry   _____   _____   _____

2. apiary   _____   _____   _____

3. legumes   _____   _____   _____

4. goobers   _____   _____   _____

5. savor   _____   _____   _____

6. garnish   _____   _____   _____

Activity: Fill in each blank with one new word.

1. There was a buzz coming from the _____ next door.

2. A bright, red cherry was the _____ on the bowl of ice cream.

3. On a winter day, hot chocolate is something to _____ .

4. _____ are a crunchy, protein-filled snack.

5. You can buy _____ fresh or in cans.

6. For dinner, we had _____ as the main course and salad as the side dish.

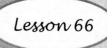

Playing the Part

Directions: Find the meaning of each underlined word in the paragraph below. Put the letter of the answer on the blank line. Use the definitions in the box below to help you.

> A. openly rude
> B. a partner
> C. to walk with a limp
> D. a long scarf
> E. behavior
> F. stolen items

1. _____
2. _____
3. _____
4. _____
5. _____
6. _____

Everyone wanted to have the lead role in the play. The teacher chose Pablo. That lucky guy! The teacher chose Pablo to play the part of the pirate. The pirate had a leg injury, so Pablo had to learn how to **1**<u>hobble</u>. He carried a large sack filled with **2**<u>loot</u> across the stage. He wore short pants, and around his loose-fitting shirt was a **3**<u>sash</u>. He was a pirate, so his attitude was **4**<u>brash</u>. His only **5**<u>mate</u> was a pet parrot on his shoulder. Pablo played the part well. He was good at showing a pirate's nasty **6**<u>demeanor</u>.

Directions: Spell each new word three times.

1. hobble _____ _____ _____

2. loot _____ _____ _____

3. sash _____ _____ _____

4. brash _____ _____ _____

5. mate _____ _____ _____

6. demeanor _____ _____ _____

Activity: Fill in each sentence with the best new word.

1. The lady and her _____ went to the park for a walk.

2. My mother told me to change my _____ or else I would be punished.

3. The very old man could only _____.

4. The girl wore a colorful, silk _____ in the parade.

5. It is not polite to be _____.

6. Where did the police find the box of _____ from the robbery?

All About Money

Directions: Use the mini dictionary to help you fill in the missing words below.

> *diner — a small restaurant*
> *handbill — a printed announcement*
> *gross — 12 dozen*
> *cinema — theater*
>
> *corral — drive animals into a pen*
> *festoon — to brightly decorate*
> *hew — to chop down*
> *bogus — fake*

Odd Jobs on Saturdays

1. Helped a farmer to _____ some dead bushes. (earned $35)

2. Helped mother to _____ the house for Christmas. (earned $15)

3. Delivered _____ all over our neighborhood. (earned $15)

4. Helped a farmer _____ his herd. (earned $35)

Where the Money Goes

5. Bought a gold watch, but I'm worried it might be _____ . (spent $45)

6. Bought a ham sandwich at the _____ . (spent $6)

7. Paid for my own ticket at the _____ . (spent $6)

8. Bought a _____ of pencils that I will share with friends. (spent $12)

Directions: Spell each new word three times.

1. diner   _____ _____ _____

2. handbills _____ _____ _____

3. gross   _____ _____ _____

4. cinema   _____ _____ _____

5. corral   _____ _____ _____

6. festoon _____ _____ _____

7. hew   _____ _____ _____

8. bogus   _____ _____ _____

Activity: On your own sheet of paper, create five sentences. Include at least one new word in each.

The Wilderness Hike

Directions: Use the mini dictionary to help you fill in the missing words in the story below.

> *culminate — to reach an end result*
> *footfall — footsteps*
> *envelop — to surround and cover*
> *desolate — empty, lonely*
> *strut — to walk proudly*
> *negligent— extremely careless*

"Your attention, hikers! We have now arrived at the most (**1.**) _____ point of this wilderness trail. Because we are the only hikers out this far, we will now turn around. In the next few minutes you might be able to hear the echo of your own (**2.**) _____. Be extra alert now, and don't do anything (**3.**) _____. I want to get you all home safely. If the late afternoon fog begins to (**4.**) _____ us, then be sure that your whistles are handy. We need to stay together and (**5.**) _____ back home with our heads held high. Oh, and did I tell you that our adventure will (**6.**) _____ with a picnic in the moonlight?"

Directions: Spell each new word three times.

1. culminate _____ _____ _____
2. footfall _____ _____ _____
3. envelop _____ _____ _____
4. desolate _____ _____ _____
5. strut _____ _____ _____
6. negligent _____ _____ _____

Activity: Create three new sentences. Use two of your new words in each sentence.

1. _____

_____

2. _____

_____

3. _____

_____

School Closed

Directions: Find the meaning of each underlined word in the newspaper article below. Put the letter of the answer on the blank line. Use the definitions in the box below to help you.

> A. to come together
> B. to check for the truth
> C. huge and horrible
> D. confusion
> E. a guard
> F. to soak through

Flooding Closes Middle School

1. _____
2. _____
3. _____
4. _____
5. _____
6. _____

Bally Middle School will remain closed for a minimum of one month. A **¹monstrous** tornado ripped off the school's roof on Thursday evening, and heavy rain flooded all of the classrooms. Inspectors say that the water will **²permeate** the floors and walls. All students and staff must remain off the school property to prevent **³disorder**. The school district will hire a **⁴sentry** to keep curious students away. The principal expects the school to reopen in April, but parents should call the office to **⁵substantiate** that. On the day the school reopens, all students must **⁶converge** at the main flagpole for an announcement.

Directions: Spell each new word three times.

1. monstrous   _____   _____   _____
2. permeate   _____   _____   _____
3. disorder   _____   _____   _____
4. sentry   _____   _____   _____
5. substantiate   _____   _____   _____
6. converge   _____   _____   _____

Activity: Fill in each blank with the new word that fits best.

1. All of the relatives will _____ for cousin Lucy's wedding.

2. Police will have to control the _____.

3. A _____ earthquake shook the whole island.

4. How can we _____ that report?

5. Watercolor paint will _____ the paper.

6. More than one _____ stands at the castle.

Thinking About Opposites

Directions: Look at the opposites described. Find the meaning of each underlined word and put the letter of the answer on the blank line.

_____ 1. a well-maintained building vs. a <u>shabby</u> place	A.	to pull back
_____ 2. quiet conversation vs. a <u>patter</u> of excitement	B.	to hold in the anger
_____ 3. to be busy vs. to sit and <u>loaf</u>	C.	broken down
_____ 4. to show great courage vs. to <u>cower</u> with fright	D.	dull and dark
_____ 5. to disagree openly vs. to <u>smolder</u> silently	E.	very skilled
_____ 6. with a bright reflection vs. very <u>opaque</u>	F.	to be lazy
_____ 7. a well-told story vs. a <u>garbled</u> report	G.	a rush of words
_____ 8. without much ability vs. very <u>proficient</u>	H.	weak
_____ 9. one individual person vs. a <u>throng</u> of people	I.	top, summit
_____ 10. a cheap shirt vs. a <u>regal</u> gown	J.	a crowd
_____ 11. good and healthy vs. quite <u>frail</u>	K.	royal
_____ 12. down on the ground vs. at the <u>zenith</u>	L.	with mixed-up words

Directions: Spell each new word three times.

1. shabby _____ _____ _____
2. patter _____ _____ _____
3. loaf _____ _____ _____
4. cower _____ _____ _____
5. smolder _____ _____ _____
6. opaque _____ _____ _____
7. garbled _____ _____ _____
8. proficient _____ _____ _____
9. throng _____ _____ _____
10. regal _____ _____ _____
11. frail _____ _____ _____
12. zenith _____ _____ _____

Activity: On a piece of paper, list your words in ABC order. Write the meaning beside each.

Riddles on the Griddle

Directions: Find the meaning of each underlined word in the riddles below. Put the letter of the answer on the blank line. Use the definitions in the box below to help you. Try to answer all of the riddles, too.

A. population
B. to twist together
C. to gallop

D. very important
E. held in prison
F. tree-lined street

_____ 1. The Amazon Rainforest in this country has millions of vines, branches, and stems that <u>entwine</u> as they grow.

_____ 2. Criminals used to be <u>incarcerated</u> on this famous island in the San Francisco Bay.

_____ 3. In Chicago, you can take a drive on a beautiful <u>boulevard</u> that follows the shore of this famous lake.

_____ 4. This small but strong breed of pony was imported from a <u>populous</u> of ponies on this island.

_____ 5. Wild horses used to <u>lope</u> freely across this Asian desert.

_____ 6. It was a <u>momentous</u> day when President Kennedy was buried in this cemetery.

Directions: Spell each new word three times.

1. entwine _____ _____ _____

2. incarcerated _____ _____ _____

3. boulevard _____ _____ _____

4. populous _____ _____ _____

5. lope _____ _____ _____

6. momentous _____ _____ _____

Activity: Draw a line to match each idea with the correct new word.

1. the opposite of "unremarkable"   A. boulevard

2. the opposite of "untangle"   B. incarcerated

3. smoother than a trail   C. populous

4. faster than a jog   D. lope

5. the opposite of being free   E. momentous

6. cities more so than towns   F. entwine

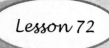

Kiss Your Cavities Goodbye

Directions: Read the following dental-health tips from your dentist. Use the mini dictionary to help you fill in the missing words.

> *pertinent — related to the point*
> *goad — to push into action*
> *culprit — the thing that caused the trouble*
>
> *fester — to decay*
> *quibble — to oppose an idea*
> *gargantuan— huge*

"It's good to see you for your regular checkup. Please relax now and sit back. Oh, dear, how can this be? I am finding a (**1.**) _____ cavity! What have you been eating since I saw you last, or haven't you been brushing?

"Listen to me carefully now. This information is very (**2.**) _____ . You need to brush often and avoid a lot of sweets. Otherwise, you'll have another tooth begin to (**3.**) _____ . I know I've told you these things before, but again I have to (**4.**) _____ you. You only have one set of teeth, and you need to keep them healthy! Watch what you eat and drink. Sugar is the real (**5.**) _____ . Please, remember, the next time your parents tell you that you are drinking too many soft drinks, don't (**6.**) _____ with them!"

Directions: Spell each new word three times.

1. pertinent   _____ _____ _____

2. goad   _____ _____ _____

3. culprit   _____ _____ _____

4. fester   _____ _____ _____

5. quibble   _____ _____ _____

6. gargantuan   _____ _____ _____

Activity: Match each of the following ideas to the correct new word. Place the letter of the answer on the blank line.

_____ 1. a mouse that ate a hole in my sock   A. quibble

_____ 2. to disagree and speak against   B. pertinent

_____ 3. to strongly encourage   C. culprit

_____ 4. the size of the Grand Canyon   D. fester

_____ 5. to become an unhealthy condition   E. gargantuan

_____ 6. necessary to know   F. goad

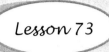

My Pocket Is Empty

Directions: Look at the advertisement below. Find the meaning of each underlined word and put the letter of the answer on the blank line. Use the definitions in the box below to help you.

> A. decorative look
> B. confusing language
> C. record-keeping book
> D. limp, droopy, without energy
> E. a fun outing or excursion
> F. a small flute

Work Wanted!

_____ 1. If your flower garden looks <u>nutant</u> because you don't have time to water it, give me a call.

_____ 2. If you are throwing a party, I can entertain your guests with my <u>fife</u>.

_____ 3. If your office is not attractive, I will help you change the <u>décor</u>.

_____ 4. If you need help with your bill paying, I can take care of your <u>ledger</u>.

_____ 5. If you are too busy to play with your children, I can take them on a <u>jaunt</u>.

_____ 6. If you can't understand your computer program, I'll teach you what the <u>jargon</u> means!

Directions: Spell each new word three times.

1. nutant _____ _____ _____

2. fife _____ _____ _____

3. décor _____ _____ _____

4. ledger _____ _____ _____

5. jaunt _____ _____ _____

6. jargon _____ _____ _____

Activity: Circle the word in each group that does not belong.

1. weak	steady	nutant	limp
2. drum	horn	shovel	fife
3. fame	décor	decoration	style
4. list	ledger	journal	invitation
5. recreation	task	adventure	jaunt
6. jargon	directions	jumble	confusion

Alien Activities

Directions: Find the meaning of each underlined word in the "alien activities" below. Put the letter of the answer on the blank line. Use the definitions in the box below to help you.

> A. a steep cliff
> B. small hills
> C. a message
>
> D. artistic
> E. foot soldiers
> F. a thick stick

_____ 1. climbing up and down the moon's gentle <u>hillocks</u>

_____ 2. marching like <u>infantry</u> on Mars

_____ 3. hang-gliding from a sharp <u>precipice</u> at the North Pole

_____ 4. hunting with a <u>cudgel</u> at the South Pole

_____ 5. photographing <u>aesthetic</u> sights in the galaxy

_____ 6. sending a <u>missive</u> to the space station

Directions: Spell each new word three times.

1. hillocks _____ _____ _____

2. infantry _____ _____ _____

3. precipice _____ _____ _____

4. cudgel _____ _____ _____

5. aesthetic _____ _____ _____

6. missive _____ _____ _____

Activity: On a separate piece of paper, use each new word in a sentence of your own. Then answer the following questions with your new vocabulary.

1. What is a simple weapon? _____

2. Where do many flowers grow? _____

3. Who fights battles? _____

4. What means the same as "lovely"? _____

5. How is information passed? _____

6. What is a dangerous spot? _____

New Words Nice and Near

Directions: Use the mini dictionary to help you complete the following sentences.

next of kin – close relatives
nicker – the sound of a horse
nurture – to raise and care for

notorious – famous in a negative way
nettle – to irritate or bother
necessitate – to make necessary

1. The condition of a house after a tornado might _____ re-building.

2. The teacher gave a strict warning that the students must not _____ each other.

3. She lives on another continent, completely separated from all of her _____.

4. When I stayed on a ranch, I was awakened each morning by a _____.

5. Facing the _____ person, the judge stayed perfectly calm.

6. A vegetable garden needs someone to _____ it.

Directions: Spell each new word or term three times.

1. next of kin   _____   _____   _____

2. nicker   _____   _____   _____

3. nurture   _____   _____   _____

4. notorious   _____   _____   _____

5. nettle   _____   _____   _____

6. necessitate   _____   _____   _____

Activity: Match each of the following ideas to the correct new word by drawing lines.

1. without good character   A. nicker

2. a sound heard in a corral   B. next of kin

3. something one should do for a baby   C. necessitate

4. people to spend the holidays with   D. notorious

5. no choice here   E. nettle

6. a disturbing action   F. nurture

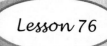

My Sister's Garden

Directions: Find the meaning of each underlined word in the paragraph below. Put the letter of the answer on the blank line. Use the definitions in the box below to help you.

> A. the end of day
> B. to spend time and effort
> C. to feel great heat
> D. motivation
> E. a small disagreement
> F. happiness

1. _____
2. _____
3. _____
4. _____
5. _____
6. _____

Mom gave my sister a space in the backyard. Tess planted her own garden there. Tess works in her garden in the heat of the summer. She **1**swelters out there in the sun, but she loves it! Sometimes, she works until **2**twilight. If Tess doesn't come into the house for dinner, she and Mom have a **3**spat about that. Tess tells Mom that it is worth it to **4**invest in her garden. To harvest big, red tomatoes is her **5**incentive. When Tess picks a tomato for our salad, she smiles with **6**glee.

Directions: Spell each new word three times.

1. swelters _____ _____ _____

2. twilight _____ _____ _____

3. spat _____ _____ _____

4. invest _____ _____ _____

5. incentive _____ _____ _____

6. glee _____ _____ _____

Activity: Draw a line to connect each idea to the correct new word.

1. definitely not sadness   A. spat

2. just before the stars come out   B. twilight

3. not a huge fight   C. swelters

4. feels the need for shade   D. invest

5. like a goal   E. glee

6. do something now to gain for the future   F. incentive

An Ocean Alien

Directions: Find the meaning of each underlined word in the paragraph below. Put the letter of the answer on the blank line. Use the definitions in the box below to help you.

> A. *to move quickly*
> B. *sneaky, sly*
> C. *to squirt out*
> D. *suspicious*
> E. *to rise*
> F. *a disturbance*

1. _____
2. _____
3. _____
4. _____
5. _____
6. _____

Most ocean creatures are completely alien to what we know on land. Both their appearance and their way of life are foreign to us. One good example of an alien creature is the octopus. It lives totally beneath the water, and nobody ever sees one **¹**ascend to the surface. The octopus is extremely **²**wily, and scuba divers have reason to fear it. The octopus has the ability to **³**spurt its own cloud to hid in. Because of its eight flexible tentacles, other creatures are **⁴**leery of it. Its eight tentacles allow it to **⁵**scuttle toward whatever meal it chooses. A battle between an octopus and its prey often creates an **⁶**agitation beneath the sea.

Directions: Spell each new word three times.

1. ascend   _____ _____ _____
2. wily   _____ _____ _____
3. spurt   _____ _____ _____
4. leery   _____ _____ _____
5. scuttle   _____ _____ _____
6. agitation   _____ _____ _____

Activity: First, put your new words in ABC order. Then write the meaning beside each new word.

1. _____ _____
2. _____ _____
3. _____ _____
4. _____ _____
5. _____ _____
6. _____ _____

The Daily News Headlines

Directions: Find the meaning of each underlined word in the headlines below. Put the letter of the answer on the blank line.

_____ 1. Heavy Rains Will <u>Saturate</u> Land		A. very hard work
_____ 2. Laboratory Develops New <u>Serum</u>		B. a wide path, track
_____ 3. Ohio Tornado Produces <u>Swath</u> of Trouble		C. to search
_____ 4. Students Say New Schedule Is <u>Drudgery</u>		D. an antibiotic
_____ 5. Detectives Will <u>Probe</u> New Case		E. relating to stars
_____ 6. <u>Astral</u> Light Measured by Telescope		F. to heavily soak
_____ 7. New Bells <u>Chime</u> at Public Park		G. a valley
_____ 8. Miners Find Huge Diamond in <u>Rubble</u>		H. an army of soldiers
_____ 9. New Civil War Book Written by <u>Historian</u>		I. pile of broken rock
_____ 10. Principal Settles Playground <u>Hubbub</u>		J. to make a ringing sound
_____ 11. Large Herd of Deer Spotted in <u>Glen</u>		K. a noisy disturbance
_____ 12. <u>Legion</u> Will Be Needed to Win War		L. an expert in history

Directions: Spell each new word three times.

1. saturate _____ _____ _____

2. serum _____ _____ _____

3. swath _____ _____ _____

4. drudgery _____ _____ _____

5. probe _____ _____ _____

6. astral _____ _____ _____

7. chime _____ _____ _____

8. rubble _____ _____ _____

9. historian _____ _____ _____

10. hubbub _____ _____ _____

11. glen _____ _____ _____

12. legion _____ _____ _____

Activity: On a separate piece of paper, create four sentences of your own. Use two new words in each sentence.

There Is More Than One Aunt

Directions: Find the meaning of each underlined word in the sentences below. Put the letter of the answer on the blank line. Use the definitions in the box below to help you.

> A. *a place to hang out or visit often*
> B. *to show off*
> C. *to make fun of someone*
> D. *thin and bony*
> E. *to brag about yourself*
> F. *a pleasure trip just for fun*

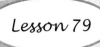

_____ 1. His friends got tired of always hearing him <u>vaunt</u>.

_____ 2. After our homework is done, let's take a <u>jaunt</u> somewhere.

_____ 3. The bowling alley is our favorite <u>haunt</u>.

_____ 4. I am worried about Grandpa. He is looking very <u>gaunt</u>.

_____ 5. It is a habit of that bully to <u>taunt</u> other people.

_____ 6. Those are very nice jeans, but don't <u>flaunt</u> them.

Directions: Spell each new word three times.

1. vaunt _____ _____ _____

2. jaunt _____ _____ _____

3. haunt _____ _____ _____

4. gaunt _____ _____ _____

5. taunt _____ _____ _____

6. flaunt _____ _____ _____

Activity: First, put all of your new words in ABC order. Then, because all of the words rhyme, write a little poem with a few of them. Use a separate piece of paper for your poem.

1. _____   4. _____

2. _____   5. _____

3. _____   6. _____

When Morning Comes

Directions: Use the mini dictionary to help you fill in the missing words in the story below.

> *dungarees — blue jeans*
> *warble — a song*
> *daybreak — dawn*
>
> *brawny — strong*
> *inclement — stormy, rainy*
> *gratitude — thankfulness*

After a good night's sleep, the rancher awakes at (**1.**) _____. He
is filled with excitement and (**2.**) _____ for another new day. He
quickly dresses in his long-sleeved shirt and dark (**3.**) _____.
After finishing his breakfast, he goes out to check the sky. He has much work to do,
and (**4.**) _____ weather would force him to delay his chores. He is
delighted to see clear skies and to hear the (**5.**) _____ of birds over his
grasslands. With a happy smile upon his face, he exercises his (**6.**) _____
muscles and gets right to work.

Directions: Spell each new word three times.

1. dungarees _____ _____ _____

2. warble _____ _____ _____

3. daybreak _____ _____ _____

4. brawny _____ _____ _____

5. inclement _____ _____ _____

6. gratitude _____ _____ _____

Activity: Copy the story from above. Include all of your new words.

_____

_____

_____

_____

_____

_____

_____

_____

_____

Stepping Into the Wilderness

Directions: The steps below offer advice on how to survive in the wilderness. As you read them, find the meaning of each underlined word and put the letter of the answer on the blank line. Use the definitions in the box below to help you.

> A. *capable*
>
> B. *sticky wetland (or troublesome situation)*
>
> C. *hidden supply*
>
> D. *to beat, hit hard*
>
> E. *blank, empty*
>
> F. *along a bank or shore*

_____ 1. First, set up your camp in a <u>riparian</u> area so that fishing is easily available.

_____ 2. Second, use the shelter of trees for your camp because a <u>stark</u> area gets too much sunshine.

_____ 3. Third, be sure that you are very <u>apt</u> at starting a campfire. You'll need it for heat and light.

_____ 4. Fourth, always have a heavy stick available in case you need to <u>drub</u> a snake.

_____ 5. Fifth, always be certain that you are walking on solid ground. To step in a <u>quagmire</u> would be dangerous!

_____ 6. Sixth, keep a <u>hoard</u> of food and water. Use it very carefully.

Directions: Spell each new word three times.

1. riparian _____ _____ _____

2. stark _____ _____ _____

3. apt _____ _____ _____

4. drub _____ _____ _____

5. quagmire _____ _____ _____

6. hoard _____ _____ _____

Activity: Complete each of the series below with one of your new words.

1. able, qualified, _____

2. coastal, mountainous, _____

3. attack, strike, _____

4. mud, muck, _____

5. storehouse, stock, _____

6. bare, nothing, _____

This Education Is Physical!

Directions: Find the meaning of each underlined word in the speech below. Put the letter of the answer on the blank line. Use the definitions in the box below to help you.

> A. adventure
> B. to damage
> C. obviously bad
> D. to stop from doing
> E. an insult
> F. lazy

1. _____

2. _____

3. _____

4. _____

5. _____

6. _____

I want to welcome all of you to the 8th grade physical education program. This will be an active program, and I don't expect anyone to be [1]idle. But, remember, not everyone has the same physical ability. You will show respect to each other, and there will be no [2]ridicule. For those of you who are stronger and faster, you must [3]refrain from boasting. All students will be respected for trying, whether or not they have great strength or speed.

I also expect all of you to respect the locker room and the equipment. Do not [4]deface anything! It is public property. Any [5]flagrant behavior will be punished.

Now, let's have fun! Let's treat each P.E. class as an [6]escapade.

Directions: Spell each new word three times.

1. idle _____ _____ _____

2. ridicule _____ _____ _____

3. refrain _____ _____ _____

4. deface _____ _____ _____

5. flagrant _____ _____ _____

6. escapade _____ _____ _____

Activity: Answer each question with the best new word.

1. Which is a cruel teasing? _____

2. Which shows no energy? _____

3. Which is a great time? _____

4. Which is restricting yourself? _____

5. Which is clearly negative? _____

6. Which means to destroy? _____

Garage Sale Stuff

Directions: Find the meaning of each underlined word and put the letter of the answer on the blank line. Use the definitions in the box below to help you.

> A. *a bell*   D. *a stamp of quality*
>
> B. *a sword*   E. *a large apron*
>
> C. *real, genuine*   F. *barrel maker*

For Sale

_____ 1. old, military <u>saber</u> (might be valuable!) — $20

_____ 2. old, wooden container (made by 19th century <u>cooper</u>) — $10

_____ 3. pretty flower vase with a <u>hallmark</u> on the bottom — $5

_____ 4. small, golden <u>timbrel</u> for Christmas time — $2

_____ 5. cotton <u>smock</u> (great for cooking projects!) — $2

_____ 6. <u>authentic</u>, autographed baseball from Wilson High's 2001 championship team! — $20

Directions: Spell each new word three times.

1. saber   _____   _____   _____

2. cooper   _____   _____   _____

3. hallmark   _____   _____   _____

4. timbrel   _____   _____   _____

5. smock   _____   _____   _____

6. authentic   _____   _____   _____

Activity: Complete each analogy with the best new word.

1. _____ is to **real** as **phony** is to **fake**

2. _____ is to **worker** as **apple** is to **fruit**

3. _____ is to **sharp** as **lemon** is to **sour**

4. _____ is to **cloth** as **window** is to **glass**

5. _____ is to **sound** as **perfume** is **smell**

6. _____ is to **product** as **symbol** is to **flag**

Mystery Mountain

Directions: Use the mini dictionary to help you fill in the missing words in the story below.

> *brambles — berry bushes*
> *belligerent — hostile*
> *sprightly — active*
>
> *mongrel — a mixed-breed dog*
> *sleuth — a detective*
> *surmise — to make a guess*

People who live on the mountain say there is a big mystery there. They report their story frequently, and it goes like this: There is a hairy (**1.**) _____ that also lives on the mountain, and people often notice that he likes to sniff the air. He sniffs and sniffs, and then he leaps about in a very quick and (**2.**) _____ way. The mountain people (**3.**) _____ that he must be smelling a rabbit, but a rabbit never appears. The other day when the hairy creature was sniffing the air, someone took a stick and poked around the (**4.**) _____. Nothing ran out, not even a rat. The behavior of the creature is not (**5.**) _____ , and people do not fear him. They are just curious about him. Whatever the creature sniffs at remains a mystery. People are talking about hiring a professional (**6.**) _____ to figure it out.

Directions: Spell each new word three times.

1. brambles _____ _____ _____

2. belligerent _____ _____ _____

3. sprightly _____ _____ _____

4. mongrel _____ _____ _____

5. sleuth _____ _____ _____

6. surmise _____ _____ _____

Activity: On a sheet of your own paper, copy the story above. Include all of the missing words.

Fun With Double Consonants

Directions: On the blank line, put the letter of the new word that best matches each definition.

_____ 1. not a gentle fight

_____ 2. short stalks (as in a cornfield)

_____ 3. to wander off

_____ 4. a small, singing bird

_____ 5. rushing water

_____ 6. a male duck

_____ 7. trash

_____ 8. a small amount of something valuable

_____ 9. confuse, jumble

_____ 10. having a rosy, red complexion

_____ 11. where a ship's cook works

_____ 12. business dealings

A. stubble

B. linnet

C. mallard

D. torrent

E. tussle

F. straggle

G. commerce

H. ruddy

I. muddle

J. rubbish

K. galley

L. nugget

Directions: Spell each new word three times.

1. stubble   _____   _____   _____

2. linnet   _____   _____   _____

3. mallard   _____   _____   _____

4. torrent   _____   _____   _____

5. tussle   _____   _____   _____

6. straggle   _____   _____   _____

7. commerce   _____   _____   _____

8. ruddy   _____   _____   _____

9. muddle   _____   _____   _____

10. rubbish   _____   _____   _____

11. galley   _____   _____   _____

12. nugget   _____   _____   _____

Activity: On a separate piece of paper, make four sentences of your own. Use two new words in each sentence you create.

When It Stormed

Directions: Find the meaning of each underlined word in the paragraph below. Put the letter of the answer on the blank line. Use the definitions in the box below to help you.

> A. *without stopping*
> B. *fearful*
> C. *to leave without rescue*
> D. *to gain the advantage*
> E. *self-control*
> F. *a wild storm*

1. _____
2. _____
3. _____
4. _____
5. _____
6. _____

We were in school yesterday when it stormed. It began with only a sprinkle of rain, so we never expected it become such a **¹**<u>tempest</u>. The sprinkles of rain soon became a downpour of rain, and then hail began to smack against the roof. It became too noisy to concentrate on our schoolwork. Instead of a brief storm, the wind and rain continued to beat on our schoolroom's windows **²**<u>incessantly</u>. Some of my classmates began to feel a bit **³**<u>apprehensive</u>. One student said, "Where will we sleep if the storm **⁴**<u>maroons</u> us here?" Our teacher then told us to keep our **⁵**<u>composure</u>. He said, "Clear skies will soon **⁶**<u>prevail</u>."

Directions: Spell each new word three time.

1. tempest _____ _____ _____
2. incessantly _____ _____ _____
3. apprehensive _____ _____ _____
4. maroon _____ _____ _____
5. composure _____ _____ _____
6. prevail _____ _____ _____

Activity: Complete each sentence with the best new word.

1. A shipwreck would _____ the sailors on a faraway island.
2. The thought of a powerful earthquake makes me feel _____.
3. A hurricane might be called a _____.
4. In order to become a master musician, one must practice _____.
5. Even in an emergency, a surgeon must keep his or her _____.
6. If you don't give up, success can _____ over failure.

Adjectives in Context

Directions: Find the meaning of each underlined word and put the letter of the answer on the blank line. Use the definitions in the box below to help you.

A. strong and healthy	D. good and kind
B. not sociable	E. embarrassed
C. cannot be heard	F. ridiculous

_____ 1. When the boy feels <u>sheepish</u>, his face turns very red.

_____ 2. A <u>benevolent</u>, rich man donated one million dollars to the charity.

_____ 3. To wear a heavy coat on a hot day would be <u>preposterous</u>.

_____ 4. Please turn up the volume; the music is nearly <u>inaudible</u>.

_____ 5. I need a <u>robust</u> person to help me move my furniture.

_____ 6. The unhappy, old man has become very <u>sullen</u>.

Directions: Spell each new word three times.

1. sheepish _____ _____ _____

2. benevolent _____ _____ _____

3. preposterous _____ _____ _____

4. inaudible _____ _____ _____

5. robust _____ _____ _____

6. sullen _____ _____ _____

Activity: Fill in each blank with one new word.

1. Good food, exercise, and plenty of sleep will make you more _____.

2. He never attends parties because he is so _____.

3. We surely need more _____ people in the world.

4. I do not agree with that _____ idea!

5. With the train passing by, the sick, old woman's voice was _____.

6. She felt so _____ about her mistake.

Shelter in a Cave

Directions: Use the mini dictionary to help you complete the story below.

> *dank — damp and chilly*
> *disdain — to have a low opinion of*
> *dilapidated — broken down*
>
> *skittish — nervous*
> *primal — primitive, base, original*
> *deluge — a sudden downpour*

It was not a bad life in a cave for those who chose to make it their home. Humans today might prefer our modern way of living, but we should not (**1.**) _____ the caveman's life. A cave is a structure that provides plenty of protection. Although it is often (**2.**) _____ inside a cave, for (**3.**) _____ man, there was great security. There was also very little to repair, so a cave never became (**4.**) _____. Cavemen did have one concern, however; they would become very (**5.**) _____ when there were heavy rains. One of their fears was being trapped in the cave due to a (**6.**) _____.

Directions: Spell each new word three times.

1. dank   _____   _____   _____

2. disdain   _____   _____   _____

3. dilapidated   _____   _____   _____

4. skittish   _____   _____   _____

5. primal   _____   _____   _____

6. deluge   _____   _____   _____

Activity: Draw a line to connect each idea to the correct new word.

1. could be a disaster   A. dank

2. the opposite of respect   B. disdain

3. not very advanced   C. deluge

4. the opposite of calm   D. dilapidated

5. like rainy weather   E. primal

6. needs rebuilding   F. skittish

The Weather—Like It or Not

Directions: Find the meaning of each underlined word in the weather headlines below. Put the letter of the answer on the blank line. Use the definitions in the box below to help you.

> A. to adjust to a change
> B. brief windstorm
> C. large and puffy
> D. great beauty
> E. persistently rough
> F. fearsome

_____ 1. A Week of <u>Grandeur</u> with Sunshine Every Day

_____ 2. High Waves on the Lake When <u>Squall</u> Passes Through

_____ 3. <u>Relentless</u> Rains Will Pound the State Next Week

_____ 4. Beautiful, <u>Billowy</u> Clouds Will Fill the Sky

_____ 5. Lovely Autumn Followed by Freezing Winter; Prepare to <u>Acclimate</u>

_____ 6. <u>Formidable</u> Tornadoes Are Expected to Form

Directions: Spell each new word three times.

1. grandeur _____ _____ _____

2. squall _____ _____ _____

3. relentless _____ _____ _____

4. billowy _____ _____ _____

5. acclimate _____ _____ _____

6. formidable _____ _____ _____

Activity: Cross out the word in each group that does not belong.

1. hurricane	tornado	earthquake	squall
2. illness	loveliness	grandeur	magnificence
3. scary	formidable	pleasant	dreadful
4. unending	continual	brief	relentless
5. billowy	oversized	huge	flat
6. arrive	acclimate	adapt	get used to

A King Named Kong

Directions: Find the meaning of each underlined word in the passage below. Put the letter of the answer on the blank line. Use the definitions in the box below to help you.

> A. *to follow with danger*
> B. *strong and heavy*
> C. *joy*
> D. *wrong*
> E. *sneaky and sly*
> F. *a very loud shout*

1. _____
2. _____
3. _____
4. _____
5. _____
6. _____

You have heard the tale of a huge and hairy ape called King Kong. Imagine the size of this **¹**burly creature! He could make buildings shake as he walked by! People lived in fear that he would **²**stalk them in their neighborhoods. He liked to capture pretty ladies, and he was very **³**furtive about doing that. If King Kong was around, there was no **⁴**mirth in town. In fact, there was a **⁵**clamor in the community to bring the police to surround him. Yes, with King Kong in town, something was definitely **⁶**amiss. There could be no law and order until King Kong was brought down.

Directions: Spell each new word three times.

1. burly _____ _____ _____
2. stalk _____ _____ _____
3. furtive _____ _____ _____
4. mirth _____ _____ _____
5. clamor _____ _____ _____
6. amiss _____ _____ _____

Activity: Draw a line from each of the following ideas to the correct new word.

1. not lightweight   A. stalk
2. a criminal action   B. amiss
3. not showing the true meaning   C. clamor
4. a great feeling   D. mirth
5. not perfect   E. furtive
6. not quiet in the least bit   F. burly

A Bit of Trivia

Directions: Find the meaning of each underlined word and put the letter of the answer on the blank line. Use the definitions in the box below to help you. How many of these trivia questions can you answer?

A. greed	D. a long journey
B. a painted picture	E. a training school
C. steam	F. a poisonous snake

_____ 1. This character's <u>avarice</u> for more and more gold did not end until even his daughter was turned to gold.

_____ 2. The explorers Lewis and Clark began their <u>trek</u> west in this year.

_____ 3. This famous queen died from the bite of a <u>serpent</u>.

_____ 4. At this <u>academy</u>, young men and women learn how to become officers in the U.S. Army.

_____ 5. The <u>vapor</u> from this hot, boiling soup helps to cure a cold.

_____ 6. At the White House, you can see the <u>portrait</u> of this movie star who became president.

Directions: Spell each new word three times.

1. avarice _____ _____ _____

2. trek _____ _____ _____

3. serpent _____ _____ _____

4. academy _____ _____ _____

5. vapor _____ _____ _____

6. portrait _____ _____ _____

Activity: Draw a line to connect each idea with the correct new word.

1. You might pose for a long time for this.   A. vapor

2. This rises into the air.   B. avarice

3. Do not get too close to this thing.   C. portrait

4. This is a place of learning.   D. trek

5. This creates selfishness.   E. academy

6. Pack plenty of supplies for this.   F. serpent

Uncle Len's Work

Directions: Find the meaning of each underlined word in the paragraph below. Put the letter of the answer on the blank line. Use the definitions in the box below to help you.

> A. *to dry up with heat*
> B. *without money*
> C. *to gather crops*
> D. *a herd of cows*
> E. *farm, agriculture*
> F. *to search for food*

1. _____
2. _____
3. _____
4. _____
5. _____
6. _____

Uncle Len lives in the state of Nebraska. His house is in the middle of wheat fields, and he earns his living in **¹**agrarian work. Besides growing wheat, he raises cows that **²**forage in the grasslands. He depends totally on getting enough rain and snow. Otherwise, his farm would fail and leave him **³**destitute. Not only his wheat, but also his **⁴**drove requires water. Last year, he was able to **⁵**reap large amounts of wheat because of good rainfall. This year, he is afraid the sun will **⁶**sear his fields.

Directions: Spell each new word three times.

1. agrarian   _____   _____   _____
2. forage   _____   _____   _____
3. destitute   _____   _____   _____
4. drove   _____   _____   _____
5. reap   _____   _____   _____
6. sear   _____   _____   _____

Activity: Fill in each blank with the best new word.

1. The rich man was known for generously giving to the _____.
2. The cowboys follow the _____ around the big ranch.
3. Is there a good profit in _____ work?
4. The farmer will sell all that he can _____.
5. Goats like to _____ on the mountainside.
6. In Spain, there is enough sun to _____ grapes into raisins.

An Important Chart

Directions: Find the meaning of each underlined word in the veterinarian's chart below. Put the letter of the answer on the blank line. Use the definitions in the box below to help you.

> A. *resistant to discipline*   D. *a low hill*
>
> B. *gloomy*   E. *to shake or tremble*
>
> C. *a thin sliver of wood*   F. *shares of food*

_____ 1. Mr. Casey's puppy has a sharp <u>splinter</u> in his paw — surgery not necessary

_____ 2. Mrs. A's cat has a high fever — will continue to <u>quaver</u> until the fever is down

_____ 3. Bob Allen's dog needs more training — is still disobedient and <u>defiant</u>

_____ 4. Mr. T's pet rabbit ate a poisonous weed on the <u>hummock</u> — condition not good

_____ 5. Jose's kitten is too fat — Jose must reduce <u>rations</u>

_____ 6. Mrs. Roth's turtle sure has a <u>glum</u> character — not a good companion for her

Directions: Spell each new p three times.

1. splinter   _____   _____   _____

2. quaver   _____   _____   _____

3. defiant   _____   _____   _____

4. hummock   _____   _____   _____

5. rations   _____   _____   _____

6. glum   _____   _____   _____

Activity: Fill in each blank below with the best new word.

1. Fear can cause a person to _____.

2. There was no cheerfulness at the _____ party.

3. The teacher sent the _____ child to the principal's office.

4. Did the hikers pack enough _____?

5. The flowers on the _____ are very colorful.

6. Your skin might bleed if you pull out the _____.

Ricardo's Dream

Directions: Find the meaning of each underlined word in the paragraphs below. Put the letter of the answer on the blank line. Use the definitions in the box below to help you.

> A. *overly proud*
> B. *modest, not vain*
> C. *permanent*
>
> D. *to regret deeply*
> E. *to think seriously about*
> F. *a skilled crafter*

1. _____

2. _____

3. _____

4. _____

5. _____

6. _____

Ricardo likes to work with his hands. During his free time, he often works with clay or mud. His uncle is a metal worker, and his father is a carpenter. Ricardo wants to be an **1**<u>artisan</u>, too. He has a dream to become a potter. When he works with clay, he creates vases and pots. He always put an **2**<u>indelible</u> mark on his pots to show that they are his own creations.

Before Ricardo begins a new pot or vase, he takes time to **3**<u>contemplate</u> the final design. That is the way he gets his best results. If he has no failure in his work, he has nothing to **4**<u>lament</u>.

Ricardo's family and friends greatly admire his creations. Most people believe that he is already a super artist, but Ricardo remains **5**<u>humble</u>. He knows that his talents are a gift in his life, but does not want to become **6**<u>arrogant</u>.

Directions: Spell each new word three times.

1. artisan   _____ _____ _____
2. indelible   _____ _____ _____
3. contemplate   _____ _____ _____
4. lament   _____ _____ _____
5. humble   _____ _____ _____
6. arrogant   _____ _____ _____

Activity: Put all of your new words in ABC order. Then, beside each word, write its meaning.

1. _____ _____
2. _____ _____
3. _____ _____
4. _____ _____
5. _____ _____
6. _____ _____

From a Tower in the Sand

Directions: Find the meaning of each underlined word in the paragraph below. Put the letter of the answer on the blank line. Use the definitions in the box below to help you.

A. persuade not to do   D. rough, unsteady

B. obey, submit   E. carelessly

C. deadly   F. joyful

1. _____

2. _____

3. _____

4. _____

5. _____

6. _____

"Your attention, please. Happy Memorial Day from your lifeguards! Today is the opening of the swimming season, and we have several important safety rules that we expect you to [1]comply with. Now, we know that everyone is [2]elated that school is out, and we do hope that you will enjoy yourselves. However, the ocean can be dangerous, and we don't want anyone rushing [3]headlong into the sea if he or she isn't a good swimmer. We do not want to completely [4]dissuade you from entering the water—just please follow these rules and you will be safe:

- Always swim with a partner.
- Swim in sight of the lifeguard tower.
- Respect the surf. It can be calm at times, but it is often [5]turbulent.
- Look out for shark fins! Sharks are [6]pernicious creatures!

Directions: Spell each new word three times.

1. comply   _____ _____ _____
2. elated   _____ _____ _____
3. headlong   _____ _____ _____
4. dissuade   _____ _____ _____
5. turbulent _____ _____ _____
6. pernicious _____ _____ _____

Activity: Circle the best answer to each of the following ideas.

1. what a good citizen will do   **dissuade** or **comply**
2. a tornado's action   **elated** or **turbulent**
3. warn, "You shouldn't do that"   **comply** or **dissuade**
4. a bat with rabies   **pernicious** or **headlong**
5. without thinking ahead   **headlong** or **elated**
6. feeling like celebrating   **turbulent** or **elated**

The Advice that Might Help You

Directions: Find the meaning of each underlined word below. Put the letter of the answer on the blank line. Use the definitions in the box below to help you.

> A. *to stray from the subject*
> B. *to hold back*
> C. *to go after*
> D. *to understand*
> E. *to put a definite end to*
> F. *to have a quarrel*

Six Bits of Advice

_____ 1. Avoid any subject that leads you to <u>bicker</u> with your friends.

_____ 2. <u>Stifle</u> your yawns whenever possible.

_____ 3. Give your book reports in an organized way, and do not <u>digress</u>.

_____ 4. <u>Strive</u> for big, new goals each day.

_____ 5. When you are reading, concentrate and try to <u>comprehend</u> everything.

_____ 6. Try to completely <u>abolish</u> any negative attitudes.

Directions: Spell each new word three times.

1. bicker _____ _____ _____

2. stifle _____ _____ _____

3. digress _____ _____ _____

4. strive _____ _____ _____

5. comprehend _____ _____ _____

6. abolish _____ _____ _____

Activity: Circle the best new word to match each idea.

1. what you can do about anger **comprehend** or **stifle**

2. when a listener might lose interest **digress** or **strive**

3. when something is over and done **abolish** or **digress**

4. when you really get it **stifle** or **comprehend**

5. sounds like an argument **abolish** or **bicker**

6. to find new challenges **bicker** or **strive**

Grandfather's Recipe

Directions: Find the meaning of each underlined word in the recipe below. Put the letter of the answer on the blank line. Use the definitions in the box below to help you.

> A. to make a bubbling sound
> B. a brief smell
> C. to breathe very hard
> D. clay
> E. a small amount
> F. a barrel

1. _____
2. _____
3. _____
4. _____
5. _____
6. _____

Take two cups of apple cider straight from the [1]keg. Pour the apple cider into a large pot and add a [2]trifle of cinnamon. From the [3]earthen jar, take a few raisins and add them to the pot. Heat the apple cider in the pot until you hear it [4]burble. Then turn down the heat, enjoy a [5]whiff, and serve a cupful. Stop drinking immediately if it makes you [6]wheeze.

Directions: Spell each new word three times.

1. keg _____ _____ _____

2. trifle _____ _____ _____

3. earthen _____ _____ _____

4. burble _____ _____ _____

5. whiff _____ _____ _____

6. wheeze _____ _____ _____

Activity: Draw a line to match each idea to the best new word.

1. not a strong odor   A. trifle

2. like dried mud   B. wheeze

3. to suffer from allergies   C. keg

4. something that holds liquid D. burble

5. when something boils   E. whiff

6. just a bit   F. earthen

Make No Mistake

Directions: Find the meaning of each underlined word and put the letter of the answer on the blank line. Use the definitions in the box below to help you.

> A. *messy writing*
>
> B. *to stay true*
>
> C. *without a plan or method*
>
> D. *to mock or make fun of*
>
> E. *words to a song*
>
> F. *to make friends again*

Class Rules

_____ 1. Rule #1: Read these rules and <u>abide</u> by them!

_____ 2. Rule #2: Be respectful of others. Do not <u>deride</u> anyone.

_____ 3. Rule #3: Type your work or print neatly. I will not accept a <u>scrawl</u>.

_____ 4. Rule #4: Using bad language or bad <u>lyrics</u> from popular music is not allowed.

_____ 5. Rule #5: Organize your papers and homework. I will not accept anything <u>haphazard</u>.

_____ 6. Rule #6: Keep the peace! If there is a disagreement, apologize and <u>reconcile</u>.

Directions: Spell each new word three times.

1. abide _____ _____ _____

2. deride _____ _____ _____

3. scrawl _____ _____ _____

4. lyrics _____ _____ _____

5. haphazard _____ _____ _____

6. reconcile _____ _____ _____

Activity: Put all of your new words in ABC order. Then, next to each word, write its meaning.

1. _____ _____

2. _____ _____

3. _____ _____

4. _____ _____

5. _____ _____

6. _____ _____

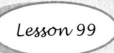

This Will Be No Picnic!

Directions: Use the mini dictionary to help you complete the story below.

resolute — with a determined mind
grubby — dirty
titan — a person of great strength

slack — loose
rote — mechanical memory
commence — to begin

"I am so happy to see so many of you signed up for this biology class. Over the next two months, you will learn more than you ever have before. After passing this class, you will be a (**1.**) _____ in this subject. In order to do this, however, you will need to be (**2.**) _____ — you cannot quit! And you won't just be learning by (**3.**) _____ — I have many creative ways of getting you to learn this information. You cannot be (**4.**) _____ and just get by without trying too hard. You will need to roll up your sleeves and do some experiments. Your hands will definitely get (**5.**) _____ once in a while! Okay, now that you understand what you are about to do, we are ready to (**6.**) _____ .

Directions: Spell each new word three times.

1. resolute   _____   _____   _____

2. grubby   _____   _____   _____

3. titan   _____   _____   _____

4. slack   _____   _____   _____

5. rote   _____   _____   _____

6. commence   _____   _____   _____

Activity: Fill in each sentence with your best new word.

1. I became so _____ from working in the garden.

2. The school year will _____ in September.

3. You will not forget if you learn by _____.

4. In order to win, you must have_____ will power.

5. His attitude yesterday was lazy and _____.

6. Hercules was certainly a _____.

What Gregory Is Known For

Directions: Find the meaning of each underlined word in the paragraph below. Put the letter of the answer on the blank line. Use the definitions in the box below to help you.

> A. *fame*
> B. *brightly joyful*
> C. *what is given*
>
> D. *able to recover*
> E. *deadly*
> F. *a worthless fellow*

1. _____

2. _____

3. _____

4. _____

5. _____

6. _____

Gregory Wells is a man of great ¹<u>renown</u>. He has achieved many honors and great success. Things did not always go nicely for him, however. When Gregory was a young college student, he took a medicine that was almost ²<u>lethal</u>. Because he was so ³<u>resilient</u>, he did survive. He became so thankful for his survival that he became absolutely ⁴<u>radiant</u>. He started each day with great optimism, and he lived each day by making important ⁵<u>contributions</u> to his community. You see, Gregory became a captain in the police force. He was a good person and never a ⁶<u>scamp</u>.

Directions: Spell each new word three times.

1. renown _____ _____ _____

2. lethal _____ _____ _____

3. resilient _____ _____ _____

4. radiant _____ _____ _____

5. contributions _____ _____ _____

6. scamp _____ _____ _____

Activity: Fill in the blank with the correct new word.

1. If you are _____ , you can get over a bad disappointment.

2. Each person needs to make _____ to the group for it to be successful.

3. The people we study from history have _____ .

4. Her _____ face showed her happiness.

5. The character is the story is really a terrible _____ .

6. The bite of a cobra can be _____ if it is not treated very quickly.

Your Attitude Needs Adjusting

Directions: Find the meaning of each word and put the letter of the answer on the blank line. Use the definitions in the box below to help you.

> A. generously kind
> B. gloomy or unhappy
> C. as a servant
> D. reckless
> E. to calm the anger
> F. sneaky, dishonest

_____ 1. You made me so mad! Now <u>placate</u> me with a nice kiss.

_____ 2. Be more careful! That was a very <u>impetuous</u> action.

_____ 3. Allow yourself to laugh! You are too <u>dour</u>.

_____ 4. How can I trust you again? Your attitude was <u>perfidious</u>.

_____ 5. I think you are selfish. Can't you be more <u>gracious</u>?

_____ 6. Your bedroom is messy, and it is not my <u>servile</u> duty to clean it for you!

Directions: Spell each new word three times.

1. placate _____ _____ _____

2. impetuous _____ _____ _____

3. dour _____ _____ _____

4. perfidious _____ _____ _____

5. gracious _____ _____ _____

6. servile _____ _____ _____

Activity: Cross out the word in each group that does not belong.

1. slave	servant	authority	servile
2. placate	aggravate	calm	smooth
3. foolish	lovely	careless	impetuous
4. dour	bright	dull	gray
5. perfidious	trustworthy	tricky	sneaky
6. hateful	gracious	loving	warm

Answer Key

Lesson 1 *(page 5)*
1. C   3. D   5. E
2. F   4. A   6. B

Activity
1. angler: fisherman
2. entice: attract
3. flair: natural talent
4. fling: to throw
5. murky: dark and unclear
6. vocation: occupation

Lesson 2 *(page 6)*
1. F   3. C   5. E
2. D   4. A   6. B

Activity
1. aghast: very frightened
2. allegiance: a loyal trust
3. bask: to enjoy some warmth
4. frond: a type of leaf
5. portent: a warning of trouble
6. rampart: a defending wall

Lesson 3 *(page 7)*
1. C   3. F   5. E
2. A   4. D   6. B

Activity
1. domain
2. deft
3. culvert
4. elm
5. smidgen
6. convivial

Lesson 4 *(page 8)*
1. B   3. A   5. C
2. F   4. D   6. E

Activity
1. rendezvous
2. tumbrel
3. implore
4. aspen
5. reprehensible
6. plenteous

Lesson 5 *(page 9)*
1. bruin
2. cumbersome
3. clad
4. sedentary
5. rouse
6. piedmont

Activity
1. sedentary
2. bruin
3. rouse
4. clad
5. piedmont
6. cumbersome

Lesson 6 *(page 10)*
1. fissure
2. steward
3. javelin
4. tirade
5. vanguard
6. panacea
7. bard
8. countenance

Activity
1. bard
2. panacea
3. vanguard
4. countenance
5. fissure
6. javelin
7. steward, tirade

Lesson 7 *(page 11)*
1. F   3. B   5. C
2. A   4. D   6. E

Activity
1. repertory
2. dismal
3. hearth
4. succor
5. bustle
6. ensemble

Lesson 8 *(page 12)*
1. B   3. F   5. A
2. D   4. C   6. E

Activity
1. forlorn   4. staid
2. skerry   5. sweep
3. serene   6. ramshackle

Lesson 9 *(page 13)*
1. leviathan
2. loll
3. erratic
4. celestial
5. maelstrom
6. prowess

Activity
1. celestial
2. maelstrom
3. erratic
4. loll
5. leviathan
6. prowess

Lesson 10 *(page 14)*
1. E   3. A   5. F
2. D   4. C   6. B

Activity
1. A   3. A   5. A
2. S   4. S   6. A

Lesson 11 *(page 15)*
1. B   3. C   5. F
2. E   4. D   6. A

Activity
1. D   3. A   5. E
2. F   4. B   6. C

Lesson 12 *(page 16)*
1. wrought   4. gaudy
2. jubilant   5. dapper
3. emulate   6. regret

Activity
1. D   3. A   5. F
2. B   4. C   6. E

Lesson 13 *(page 17)*
1. D   3. A   5. E
2. B   4. F   6. C

Activity
1. B   3. D   5. C
2. F   4. A   6. E

Lesson 14 *(page 18)*
1. E   3. B   5. F
2. D   4. A   6. C

Activity
1. breeches
2. calamity
3. adroit
4. aversion
5. wranglers
6. perseverance

Lesson 15 *(page 19)*
1. B   3. A   5. D
2. C   4. E   6. F

Activity
1. mean   4. prairie
2. intelligence   5. fortunes
3. task   6. resist

Lesson 16 *(page 20)*
1. F   3. E   5. D
2. B   4. A   6. C

Activity
1. carriage: posture
2. clash: to disagree
3. insidious: sneaky, tricky
4. invectives: bad words
5. stickler: a strict person
6. sulk: to appear angry

Lesson 17 *(page 21)*
1. E   3. D   5. B
2. A   4. C   6. F

Activity
1. E   3. D   5. B
2. A   4. C   6. F

Lesson 18 *(page 22)*
1. stow   4. pall
2. queasy   5. actuate
3. blithe   6. fruition

Lesson 19 *(page 23)*
1. C   3. E   5. B
2. F   4. A   6. D

Activity
1. S   3. S   5. A
2. A   4. A   6. A

Lesson 20 *(page 24)*
1. B   3. A   5. F
2. D   4. C   6. E

Activity
1. elude
2. conveyance
3. malevolent
4. ramble
5. feckless
6. denizen

Lesson 21 *(page 25)*
1. C   3. A   5. D
2. B   4. F   6. E

Activity
1. sentinel   4. lunge
2. irk   5. ornery
3. caper   6. protrude

Lesson 22 *(page 26)*
1. F   3. A   5. E
2. D   4. B   6. C

Activity
1. hide, Y   4. attract, Y
2. boring, N   5. swarm, Y
3. crowd, N   6. royal, Y

Lesson 23 *(page 27)*
1. B   3. E   5. A
2. F   4. C   6. D

Activity
1. simple   4. election
2. canine   5. purchase
3. task   6. duty

Lesson 24 *(page 28)*
1. C   3. D   5. F
2. A   4. B   6. E

Activity
1. brew: fruit tea or punch
2. marmalade: orange jam
3. palette: painter's color board
4. raven: crow, blackbird
5. receptacle: container
6. thicket: where bushes grow

Lesson 25 *(page 29)*
1. B   5. D   9. J
2. F   6. C   10. I
3. E   7. K   11. G
4. A   8. L   12. H

Lesson 26 *(page 30)*
1. B   3. C   5. E
2. D   4. F   6. A

Answer Key *(cont.)*

Activity
1. E　　3. B　　5. C
2. A　　4. F　　6. D

Lesson 27 *(page 31)*
1. E　　3. A　　5. C
2. D　　4. F　　6. B

Activity
1. manacles
2. turmoil
3. careen
4. promontory
5. marsh
6. thwart

Lesson 28 *(page 32)*
1. E　　5. C　　9. L
2. D　　6. B　　10. G
3. F　　7. H　　11. K
4. A　　8. J　　12. I

Lesson 29 *(page 33)*
1. F　　3. A　　5. D
2. B　　4. E　　6. C

Activity
1. garb
2. impeccable
3. peer
4. compile
5. cipher
6. affable

Lesson 30 *(page 34)*
1. salvage　　4. assure
2. tamper　　5. reserve
3. decrepit　　6. furnish

Activity
1. reserve　　4. decrepit
2. assure　　5. tamper
3. furnish　　6. salvage

Lesson 31 *(page 35)*
1. B　　3. A　　5. C
2. F　　4. E　　6. D

Activity
1. squander　　4. duplicity
2. tranquility　　5. ignominy
3. glower　　6. injurious

Lesson 32 *(page 36)*
1. E　　4. D
2. B　　5. F
3. C　　6. A

Activity
1. ravine　　4. sylvan
2. tuft　　5. sanctuary
3. ophidian　　6. stealth

Lesson 33 *(page 37)*
1. F　　3. C　　5. A
2. B　　4. D　　6. E

Activity
1. underbrush
2. aspire
3. crude
4. flourish
5. intrepid
6. membranes

Lesson 34 *(page 38)*
1. E　　3. D　　5. F
2. B　　4. A　　6. C

Activity
1. expedient
2. plethora
3. venerable
4. pillar
5. abode
6. incomparable

Lesson 35 *(page 39)*
1. D　　3. F　　5. A
2. C　　4. B　　6. E

Activity
1. B　　3. C　　5. D
2. A　　4. E　　6. F

Lesson 36 *(page 40)*
1. pelt
2. tawny
3. treacherous
4. deliberate
5. frayed
6. humiliation

Lesson 37 *(page 41)*
1. B　　4. G　　7. H
2. C　　5. E　　8. D
3. F　　6. A

Lesson 38 *(page 42)*
1. C　　3. D　　5. A
2. E　　4. B　　6. F

Activity
1. F　　3. A　　5. D
2. E　　4. B　　6. C

Lesson 39 *(page 43)*
1. C　　5. D　　9. L
2. E　　6. F　　10. K
3. A　　7. I　　11. H
4. B　　8. J　　12. G

Lesson 40 *(page 44)*
1. E　　3. B　　5. D
2. C　　4. A　　6. F

Activity
1. frenzy　　4. avail
2. remorse　　5. succumb
3. torrid　　6. blunder

Lesson 41 *(page 45)*
1. B　　3. C　　5. E
2. A　　4. D　　6. F

Activity
1. discontent: not satisfied
2. jovial: jolly
3. sundry: many, various
4. transfigures: to change or transform
5. visage: a person's face
6. yearn: to wish or dream

Lesson 42 *(page 46)*
1. F　　3. E　　5. B
2. C　　4. A　　6. D

Activity
1. C　　3. F　　5. D
2. A　　4. E　　6. B

Lesson 43 *(page 47)*
1. confound
2. mustang
3. wallow
4. colossal
5. critters
6. inception

Activity
1. confound
2. wallow
3. mustang
4. colossal
5. inception
6. critters

Lesson 44 *(page 48)*
1. E　　3. A　　5. C
2. D　　4. F　　6. B

Activity
1. knave
2. trinket
3. venue
4. mastiff
5. sprint
6. protagonist

Lesson 45 *(page 49)*
1. F　　3. E　　5. B
2. D　　4. C　　6. A

Activity
1. ungainly　　4. crag
2. surge　　5. apex
3. resolve　　6. dubious

Lesson 46 *(page 50)*
1. B　　3. A　　5. C
2. E　　4. F　　6. D

Activity
1. F　　3. E　　5. B
2. C　　4. A　　6. D

Lesson 47 *(page 51)*
1. yearn
2. downhearted
3. valiant
4. requisite
5. defunct
6. courier

Lesson 48 *(page 52)*
1. C: California
2. E: China
3. D: Milky Way
4. B: Yellowstone
5. A: Beauty and the Beast
6. F: Alexander Bell

Activity
1. belle
2. saga
3. incredulous
4. din
5. nebulous
6. detained

Lesson 49 *(page 53)*
1. C　　3. A　　5. E
2. B　　4. D　　6. F

Activity
1. embark
2. fleeting
3. humdrum
4. delineate
5. captivating
6. cognizant

Lesson 50 *(page 54)*
1. D　　3. B　　5. C
2. E　　4. F　　6. A

Activity
1. hominy　　4. gherkins
2. cask　　5. tantalize
3. pungent　　6. mutton

Lesson 51 *(page 55)*
1. D　　3. C　　5. F
2. A　　4. B　　6. E

Activity
1. hapless　　4. aerial
2. osprey　　5. rills
3. ferocity　　6. meager

Lesson 52 *(page 56)*
1. F　　3. A　　5. C
2. D　　4. E　　6. B

Activity
1. plunder
2. buccaneer
3. skirmish
4. stance
5. flinch
6. appeal

Lesson 53 *(page 57)*
1. B
2. F
3. H
4. A
5. G
6. E
7. D
8. C

Activity
1. chronicle
2. bangle
3. blemish
4. chard
5. apparition
6. bounty
7. flotsam
8. conflagration

Lesson 54 *(page 58)*
1. B
2. A
3. C
4. E
5. F
6. D

Activity
1. ardor: excited interest
2. deficient: lacking in amount
3. intricate: complicated
4. opulent: with a lot of luxury
5. purvey: to supply
6. skeptic: a disbeliever

Lesson 55 *(page 59)*
1. B
2. D
3. A
4. C
5. E
6. F

Activity
1. murex
2. maverick
3. motif
4. menace
5. malady
6. maraud

Lesson 56 *(page 60)*
1. scrupulous
2. perusal
3. omniscient
4. perplex
5. sappy
6. clarity

Activity
1. A
2. C
3. E
4. B
5. F
6. D

Lesson 57 *(page 61)*
1. Statesman
2. Phantasma
3. Insignia
4. Hideous
5. Firelock
6. Baron

Activity
1. E
2. F
3. A
4. D
5. B
6. C

Lesson 58 *(page 62)*
1. plumage
2. diffident
3. bog
4. ploy
5. defray
6. revel

Activity
1. bog: swamp, marsh
2. defray: to pay the cost
3. diffident: shy
4. ploy: a clever trick
5. plumage: set of feathers
6. revel: to celebrate

Lesson 59 *(page 63)*
1. premiere
2. despot
3. cavalcade
4. tribulation
5. toupee
6. bunker
7. testimony
8. correspondent

Activity
1. despot
2. bunker
3. premiere
4. toupee
5. tribulation
6. cavalcade
7. correspondent
8. testimony

Lesson 60 *(page 64)*
1. A
2. D
3. B
4. C
5. F
6. E

Lesson 61 *(page 65)*
1. B
2. E
3. A
4. D
5. C
6. F

Activity
1. solicitude
2. memorable
3. confidential
4. dingy
5. unblemished
6. shearling

Lesson 62 *(page 66)*
1. unfurl
2. fliers
3. paramount
4. adhere
5. diligent
6. unruly

Activity
1. fliers
2. adhere
3. diligent
4. paramount
5. unfurl
6. unruly

Lesson 63 *(page 67)*
1. C
2. E
3. F
4. B
5. A
6. D
7. G
8. H
9. K
10. L
11. J
12. I

Lesson 64 *(page 68)*
1. D
2. F
3. E
4. C
5. A
6. B

Activity
1. C
2. D
3. A
4. B
5. F
6. E

Lesson 65 *(page 69)*
1. D
2. C
3. E
4. F
5. B
6. A

Activity
1. apiary
2. garnish
3. savor
4. Goobers
5. legumes
6. poultry

Lesson 66 *(page 70)*
1. C
2. F
3. D
4. A
5. B
6. E

Activity
1. mate
2. demeanor
3. hobble
4. sash
5. brash
6. loot

Lesson 67 *(page 71)*
1. hew
2. festoon
3. handbills
4. corral
5. bogus
6. diner
7. cinema
8. gross

Lesson 68 *(page 72)*
1. desolate
2. footfall
3. negligent
4. envelop
5. strut
6. culminate

Lesson 69 *(page 73)*
1. C
2. F
3. D
4. E
5. B
6. A

Activity
1. converge
2. disorder
3. monstrous
4. substantiate
5. permeate
6. sentry

Lesson 70 *(page 74)*
1. C
2. G
3. F
4. A
5. B
6. D
7. L
8. E
9. J
10. K
11. H
12. I

Activity
1. cower: to pull back
2. frail: weak
3. garbled: with mixed-up words
4. loaf: to be lazy
5. opaque: dull, dark
6. patter: a rush of words
7. proficient: very skilled
8. regal: royal
9. shabby: broken down
10. smolder: hold in the anger
11. throng: a crowd
12. zenith: top, summit

Lesson 71 *(page 75)*
1. B: Brazil
2. E: Alcatraz
3. F: Lake Michigan
4. A: Shetland Island
5. C: Gobi Desert
6. D: Arlington National Cemetery

Activity
1. E
2. F
3. A
4. D
5. B
6. C

Lesson 72 *(page 76)*
1. gargantuan
2. pertinent
3. fester
4. goad
5. culprit
3. quibble

Activity
1. C
2. A
3. F
4. E
5. D
6. B

Lesson 73 *(page 77)*
1. D
2. F
3. A
4. C
5. E
6. B

Activity
1. steady
2. shovel
3. fame
4. invitation
5. task
6. directions

Lesson 74 *(page 78)*
1. B
2. E
3. A
4. F
5. D
6. C

Activity
1. cudgel
2. hillocks
3. infantry
4. aesthetic
5. missive
6. precipice

Lesson 75 *(page 79)*
1. necessitate
2. nettle
3. next of kin
4. nicker
5. notorious
6. nurture

Activity
1. D
2. A
3. F
4. B
5. C
6. E

Lesson 76 *(page 80)*
1. C
2. A
3. E
4. B
5. D
6. F

Activity
1. E
2. B
3. A
4. C
5. F
6. D

Lesson 77 *(page 81)*
1. E
2. B
3. C
4. D
5. A
6. F

Activity
1. agitation: a disturbance
2. ascend: to rise
3. leery: suspicious
4. scuttle: to move quickly
5. spurt: to squirt out
6. wily: sneaky, sly

Lesson 78 *(page 82)*
1. F
2. D
3. B
4. A
5. C
6. E
7. J
8. I
9. L
10. K
11. G
12. H

Answer Key *(cont.)*

Lesson 79 *(page 83)*

1. E	3. A	5. C
2. F	4. D	6. B

Activity
1. flaunt
2. gaunt
3. haunt
4. jaunt
5. taunt
6. vaunt

Lesson 80 *(page 84)*
1. daybreak
2. gratitude
3. dungarees
4. inclement
5. warble
6. brawny

Lesson 81 *(page 85)*

1. F	3. A	5. B
2. E	4. D	6. C

Activity
1. apt
2. riparian
3. drub
4. quagmire
5. hoard
6. stark

Lesson 82 *(page 86)*

1. F	3. D	5. C
2. E	4. B	6. A

Activity
1. ridicule
2. idle
3. escapade
4. refrain
5. flagrant
6. deface

Lesson 83 *(page 87)*

1. B	3. D	5. E
2. F	4. A	6. C

Activity
1. authentic
2. cooper
3. saber
4. smock
5. timbrel
6. hallmark

Lesson 84 *(page 88)*
1. mongrel
2. sprightly
3. surmise
4. brambles
5. belligerent
6. sleuth

Lesson 85 *(page 89)*

1. E	5. D	9. I
2. A	6. C	10. H
3. F	7. J	11. K
4. B	8. L	12. G

Lesson 86 *(page 90)*

1. F	3. B	5. E
2. A	4. C	6. D

Activity
1. maroon
2. apprehensive
3. tempest
4. incessantly
5. composure
6. prevail

Lesson 87 *(page 91)*

1. E	3. F	5. A
2. D	4. C	6. B

Activity
1. robust
2. sullen
3. benevolent
4. preposterous
5. inaudible
6. sheepish

Lesson 88 *(page 92)*
1. disdain
2. dank
3. primal
4. dilapidated
5. skittish
6. deluge

Activity

1. C	3. E	5. A
2. B	4. F	6. D

Lesson 89 *(page 93)*

1. D	3. E	5. A
2. B	4. C	6. F

Activity
1. earthquake
2. illness
3. pleasant
4. brief
5. flat
6. arrive

Lesson 90 *(page 94)*

1. B	3. E	5. F
2. A	4. C	6. D

Activity

1. F	3. E	5. B
2. A	4. D	6. C

Lesson 91 *(page 95)*
1. A: King Midas
2. D: 1802
3. F: Cleopatra
4. E: West Point
5. C: chicken soup
6. B: Ronald Reagan

Activity

1. C	3. F	5. B
2. A	4. E	6. D

Lesson 92 *(page 96)*

1. E	3. B	5. C
2. F	4. D	6. A

Activity
1. destitute
2. drove
3. agrarian
4. reap
5. forage
6. sear

Lesson 93 *(page 97)*

1. C	3. A	5. F
2. E	4. D	6. B

Activity
1. quaver
2. glum
3. defiant
4. rations
5. hummock
6. splinter

Lesson 94 *(page 98)*

1. F	3. E	5. B
2. C	4. D	6. A

Activity
1. arrogant: overly proud
2. artisan: a skilled crafter
3. contemplate: to think seriously about
4. humble: modest, not overly proud
5. indelible: permanent
6. lament: to regret deeply

Lesson 95 *(page 99)*

1. B	3. E	5. D
2. F	4. A	6. C

Activity
1. comply
2. turbulent
3. dissuade
4. pernicious
5. headlong
6. elated

Lesson 96 *(page 100)*

1. F	3. A	5. D
2. B	4. C	6. E

Activity
1. stifle
2. digress
3. abolish
4. comprehend
5. bicker
6. strive

Lesson 97 *(page 101)*

1. F	3. D	5. B
2. E	4. A	6. C

Activity

1. E	3. B	5. D
2. F	4. C	6. A

Lesson 98 *(page 102)*

1. B	3. A	5. C
2. D	4. E	6. F

Activity
1. abide: to stay true
2. deride: to mock or make fun of
3. haphazard: without a plan or method
4. lyrics: words to a song
5. reconcile: to make friends again
6. scrawl: messy writing

Lesson 99 *(page 103)*
1. titan
2. resolute
3. rote
4. slack
5. grubby
6. commence

Activity
1. grubby
2. commence
3. rote
4. resolute
5. slack
6. titan

Lesson 100 *(page 104)*

1. A	3. D	5. C
2. E	4. B	6. F

Activity
1. resilient
2. contribution
3. renown
4. radiant
5. scamp
6. lethal

Lesson 101 *(page 105)*

1. E	3. B	5. A
2. D	4. F	6. C

Activity
1. authority
2. aggravate
3. lovely
4. bright
5. trustworthy
6. hateful

Word Index—By Page Number

Word Index—By Page Number *(cont.)*

Word Index—By Page Number *(cont.)*